STUDENT LECTURE NOTEBOOK

FOUNDATIONS OF
EARTH
SCIENCE

FOURTH EDITION

Lutgens • Tarbuck

Upper Saddle River, NJ 07458

Editor-in-Chief, Science: John Challice
Executive Editor: Patrick Lynch
Assistant Editor: Melanie Cutler
Vice President of Production & Manufacturing: David W. Riccardi
Executive Managing Editor: Kathleen Schiaparelli
Assistant Managing Editor: Becca Richter
Production Editor: Elizabeth Klug
Supplement Cover Manager: Paul Gourhan
Supplement Cover Designer: Joanne Alexandris
Manufacturing Buyer: Ilene Kahn
Cover Photo Credit: Digital Vision/Berg Lake and Mount Robson, British Columbia, Canada

© 2005   Pearson Education, Inc.
Pearson Prentice Hall
Pearson Education, Inc.
Upper Saddle River, NJ 07458

The author and publisher of this book have used their best efforts in preparing this book. These efforts include the development, research, and testing of the theories and programs to determine their effectiveness. The author and publisher make no warranty of any kind, expressed or implied, with regard to these programs or the documentation contained in this book. The author and publisher shall not be liable in any event for incidental or consequential damages in connection with, or arising out of, the furnishing, performance, or use of these programs.

Printed in the United States of America

10   9   8   7   6   5   4   3   2   1

ISBN 0-13-144762-9

Pearson Education Ltd., *London*
Pearson Education Australia Pty. Ltd., *Sydney*
Pearson Education Singapore, Pte. Ltd.
Pearson Education North Asia Ltd., *Hong Kong*
Pearson Education Canada, Inc., *Toronto*
Pearson Educación de Mexico, S.A. de C.V.
Pearson Education—Japan, *Tokyo*
Pearson Education Malaysia, Pte. Ltd.

Contents

To the Student

This *Student Lecture Notebook* is designed to help you do your best in this Earth science course.

Key images from the textbook and every illustration from the Instructor's Transparency Set are reproduced in this notebook. Because you won't have to redraw the art in class, you can focus your attention on the lecture, annotate the art, and take your notes in this book.

Leave all your notes together or remove them for integration into a binder with other course materials.

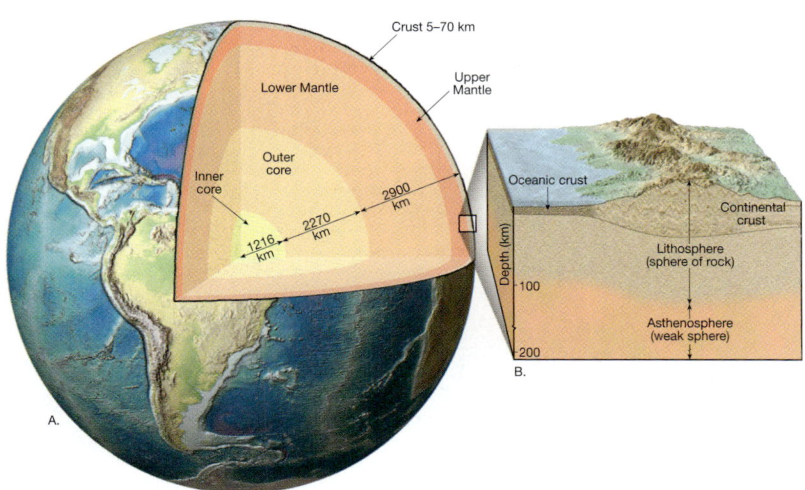

Figure I.4 **View of Earth's layered structure.**

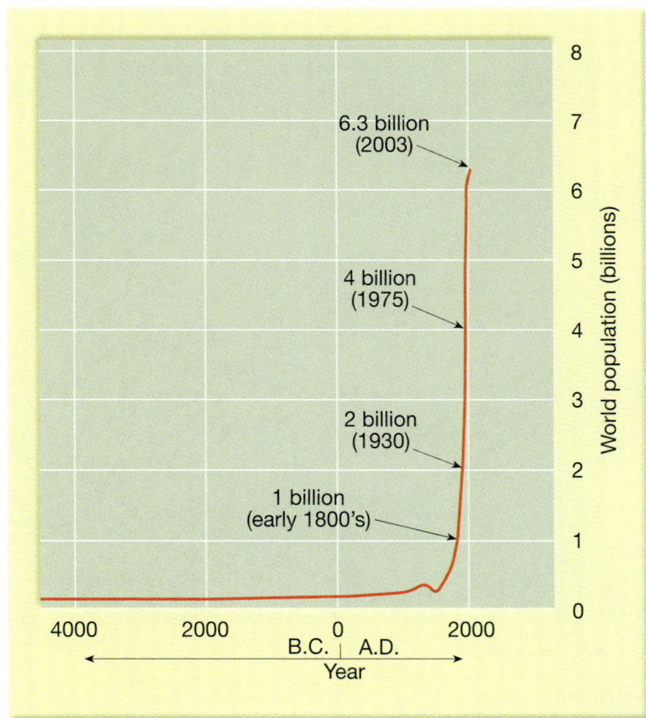

Figure I.9 **Growth of world population.**

NOTES:

Photo by E.J. Tarbuck   Photos courtesy AGI

Figure 1.3 Rocks are aggregates of one or more minerals.

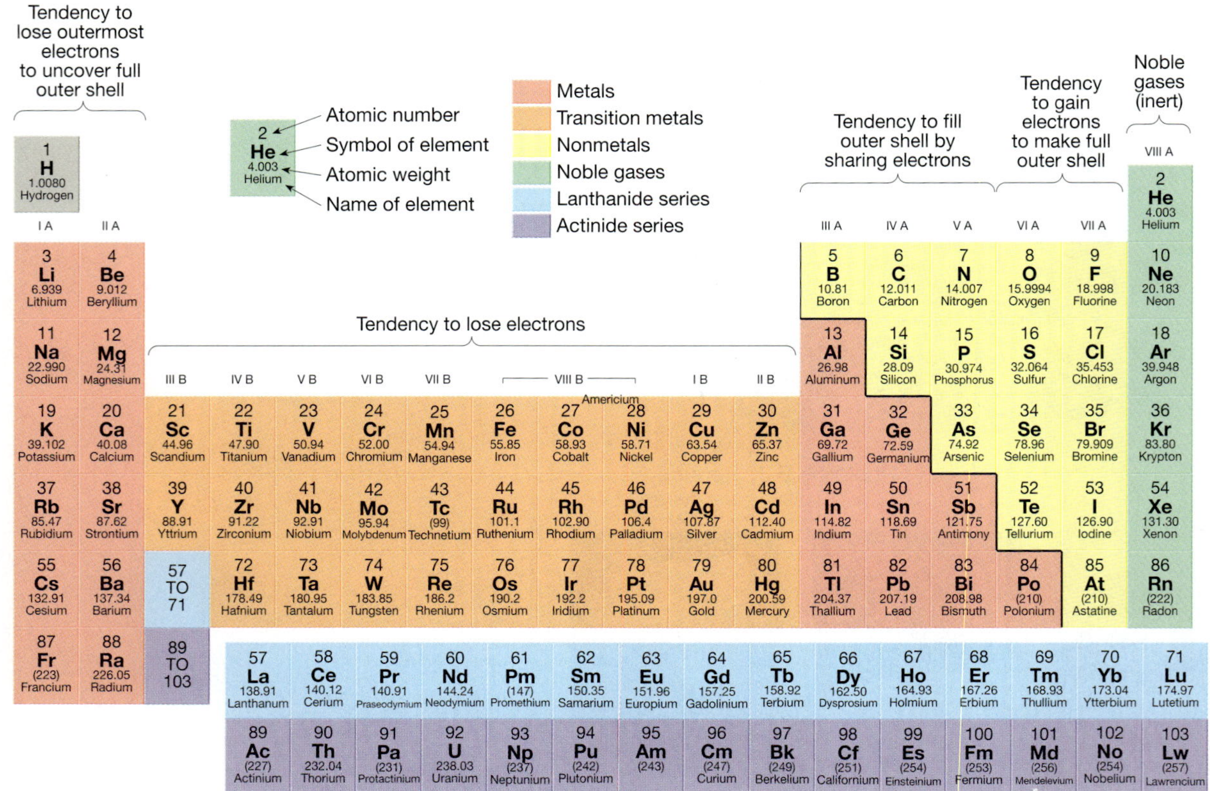

Figure 1.4 Periodic Table of the Elements.

NOTES:

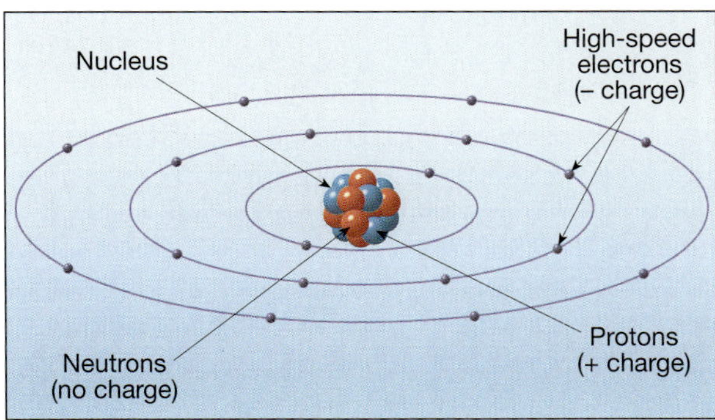

A.

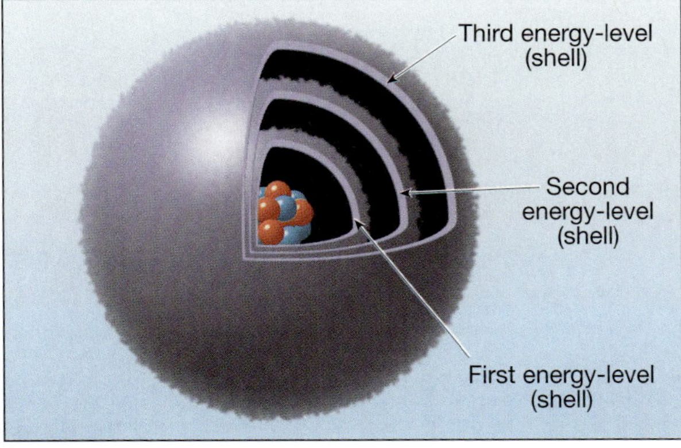

B.

Figure 1.5 Two models of the atom.

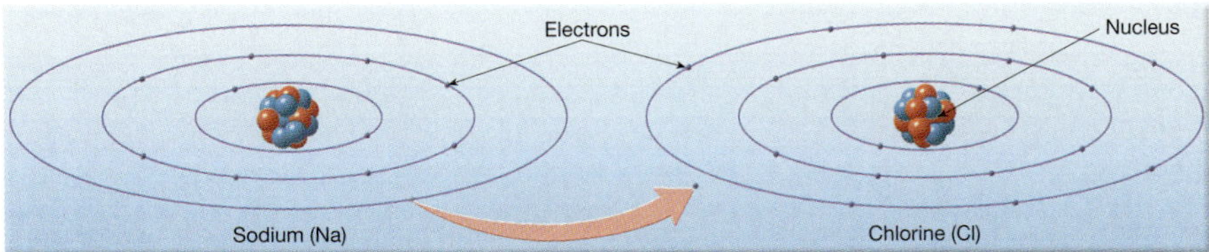

Figure 1.6 Chemical bonding of sodium and chlorine atoms to produce sodium chloride.

NOTES:

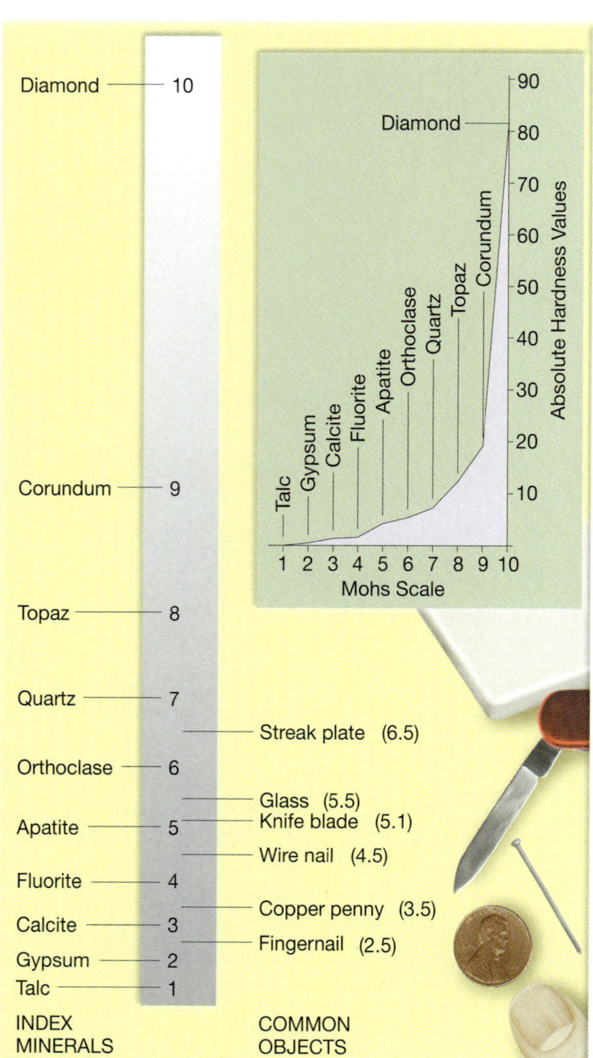

Figure 1.9 Mohs scale of hardness.

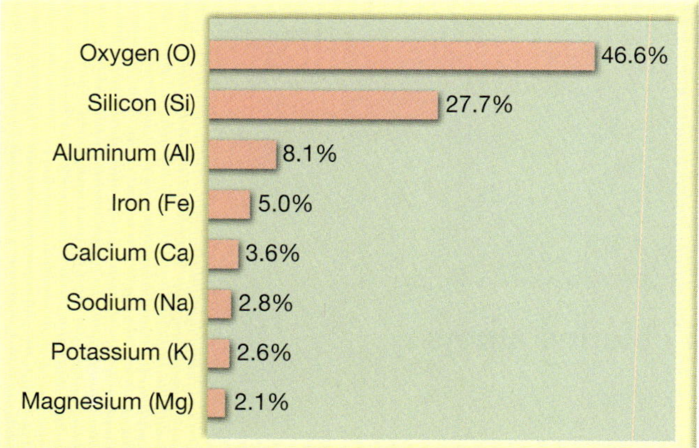

Figure 1.14 Relative abundance of the eight most abundant elements in the continental crust.

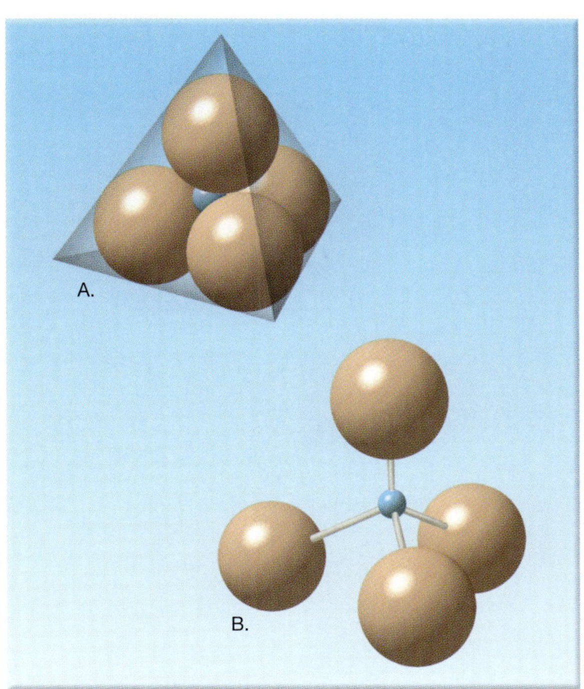

Figure 1.15 Two representations of the silicon-oxygen tetrahedron.

Mineral		Idealized Formula	Cleavage	Silicate Structure	
Olivine		$(Mg, Fe)_2SiO_4$	None	Single tetrahedron	
Pyroxene group (Augite)		$(Mg,Fe)SiO_3$	Two planes at right angles	Single chains	
Amphibole group (Hornblende)		$Ca_2(Fe,Mg)_5Si_8O_{22}(OH)_2$	Two planes at 60° and 120°	Double chains	
Micas	Biotite	$K(Mg,Fe)_3AlSi_3O_{10}(OH)_2$	One plane	Sheets	
	Muscovite	$KAl_2(AlSi_3O_{10})(OH)_2$			
Feldspars	Potassium feldspar (Orthoclase)	$KAlSi_3O_8$	Two planes at 90°	Three-dimensional networks	
	Plagioclase	$(Ca,Na)AlSi_3O_8$			
Quartz		SiO_2	None		

Figure 1.16 Common silicate minerals.

Photos courtesy Ed Tarbuck and AGI

Figure 1.17 Common rock-forming minerals.

NOTES:

NOTES:

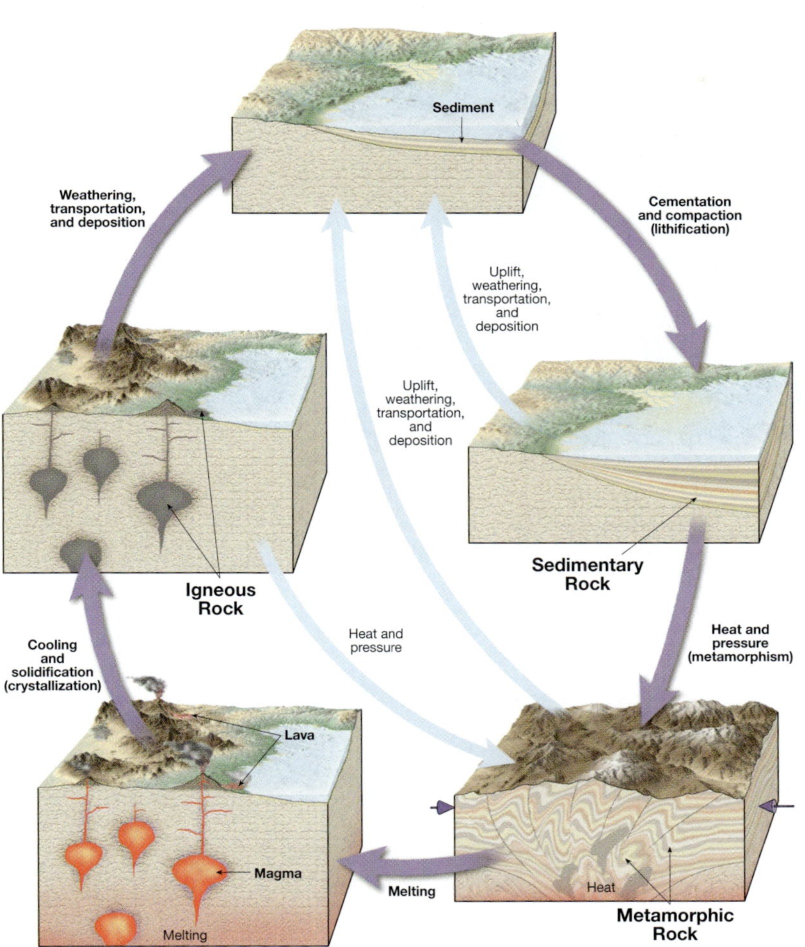

Figure 2.2 The rock cycle.

Chemical Composition		Granitic (Felsic)	Andesitic (Intermediate)	Basaltic (Mafic)	Ultramafic
Dominant Minerals		Quartz Potassium feldspar Sodium-rich plagioclase feldspar	Amphibole Sodium- and calcium-rich plagioclase feldspar	Pyroxene Calcium-rich plagioclase feldspar	Olivine Pyroxene
T E X T U R E	Phaneritic (coarse-grained)	Granite	Diorite	Gabbro	Peridotite
	Aphanitic (fine-grained)	Rhyolite	Andesite	Basalt	Komatiite (rare)
	Porphyritic	"Porphyritic" precedes any of the above names whenever there are appreciable phenocrysts			Uncommon
	Glassy	Obsidian (compact glass) Pumice (frothy glass)			
Rock Color (based on % of dark minerals)		0% to 25%	25% to 45%	45% to 85%	85% to 100%

Figure 2.8 Classification of igneous rocks.

NOTES:

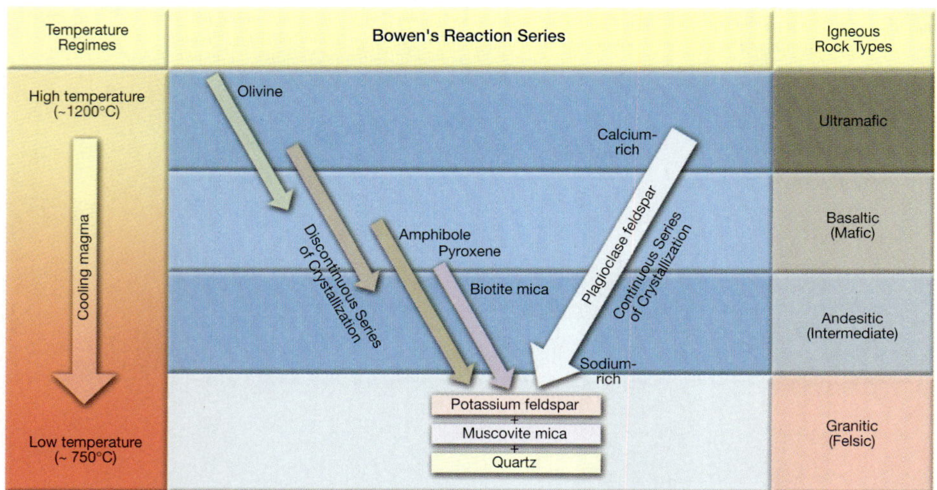

Figure 2.9 Bowen's reaction series.

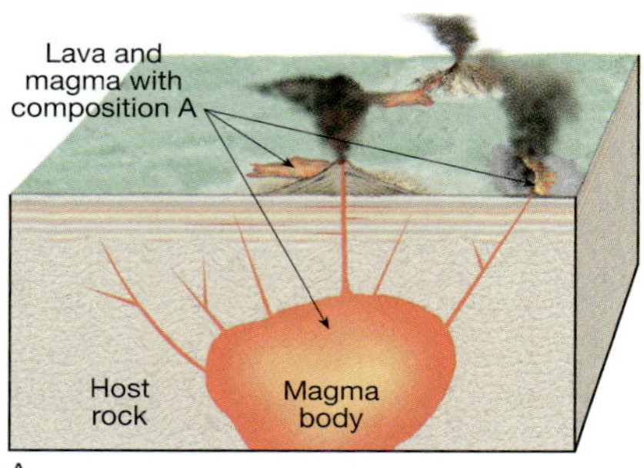

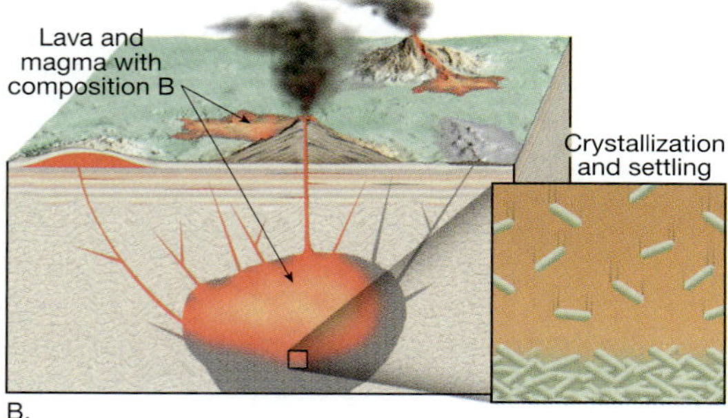

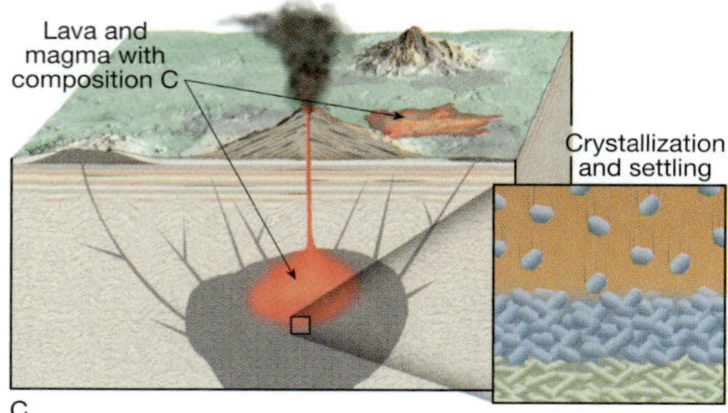

Figure 2.10 Evolution of a magma.

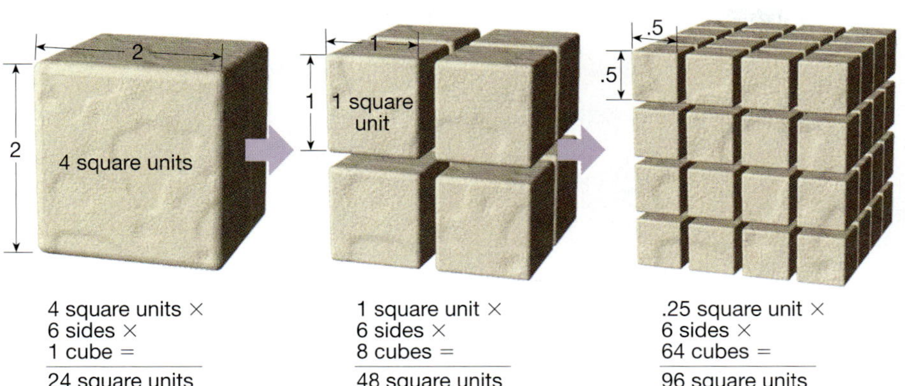

4 square units ×
6 sides ×
1 cube =
24 square units

1 square unit ×
6 sides ×
8 cubes =
48 square units

.25 square unit ×
6 sides ×
64 cubes =
96 square units

Figure 2.11 Mechanical weathering increases exposed surface area.

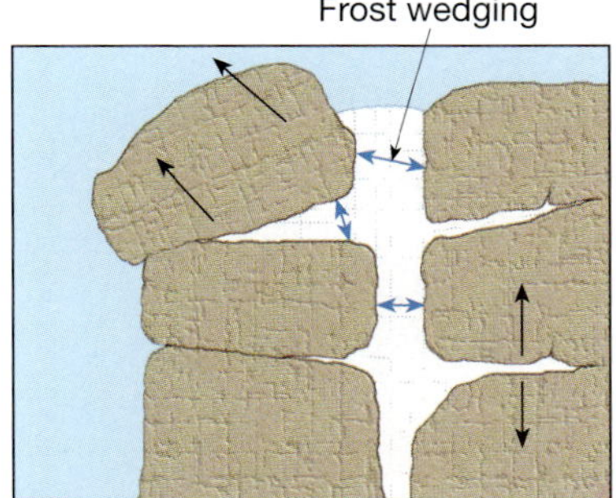

Figure 2.12 Frost wedging.

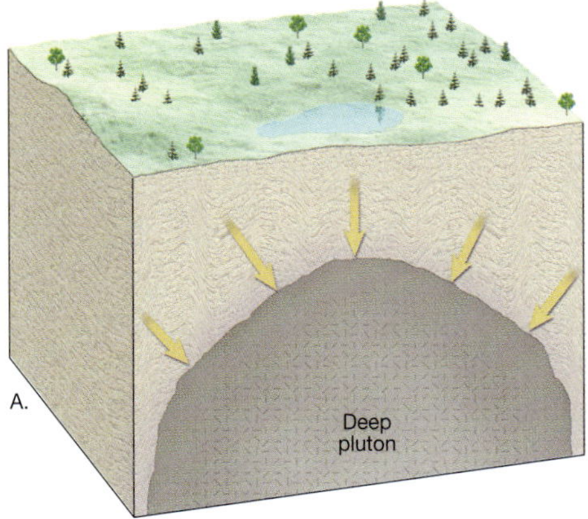

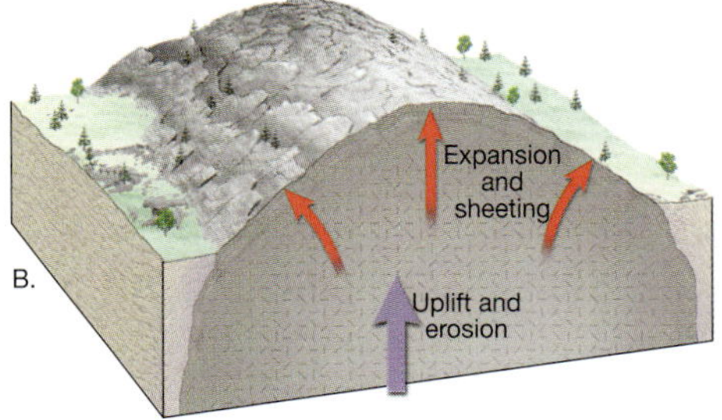

Figure 2.13 A,B Sheeting.

NOTES:

Detrital Sedimentary Rocks				Chemical Sedimentary Rocks		
Clastic Texture Particle Size		Sediment Name	Rock Name	Composition	Texture	Rock Name
Coarse (over 2 mm)		Gravel (Rounded particles)	Conglomerate	Calcite, $CaCO_3$	Nonclastic: Fine to coarse crystalline	Crystalline Limestone
		Gravel (Angular particles)	Breccia			Travertine
Medium (1/16 to 2 mm)		Sand (If abundant feldspar is present the rock is called **Arkose**)	Sandstone		Clastic: Visible shells and shell fragments loosely cemented	Coquina
					Clastic: Various size shells and shell fragments cemented with calcite cement	Fossiliferous Limestone
Fine (1/16 to 1/256 mm)		Mud	Siltstone		Clastic: Microscopic shells and clay	Chalk
Very fine (less than 1/256 mm)		Mud	Shale	Quartz, SiO_2	Nonclastic: Very fine crystalline	Chert (light colored) Flint (dark colored)
				Gypsum $CaSO_4 \cdot 2H_2O$	Nonclastic: Fine to coarse crystalline	Rock Gypsum
				Halite, NaCl	Nonclastic: Fine to coarse crystalline	Rock Salt
				Altered plant fragments	Nonclastic: Fine-grained organic matter	Bituminous Coal

(Coquina, Fossiliferous Limestone, and Chalk are grouped as **Biochemical Limestone**.)

Figure 2.16 **Identification of sedimentary rocks.**

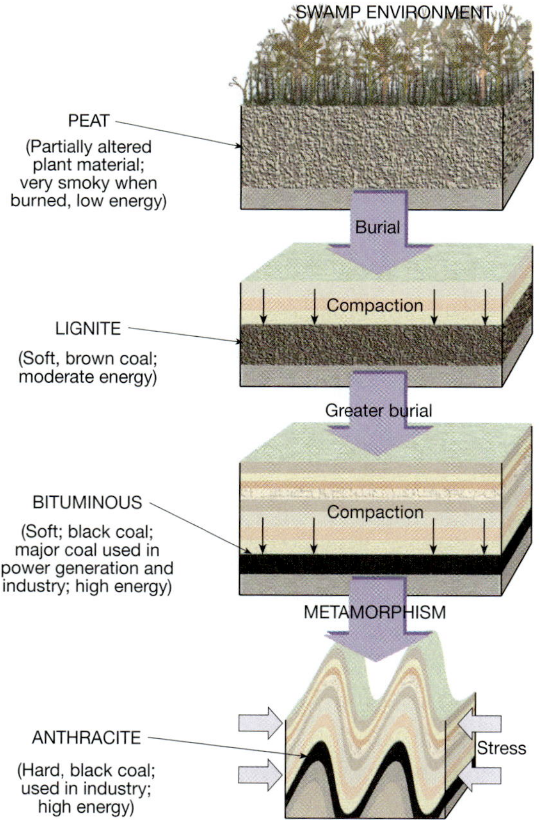

Figure 2.21 **Stages in coal formation.**

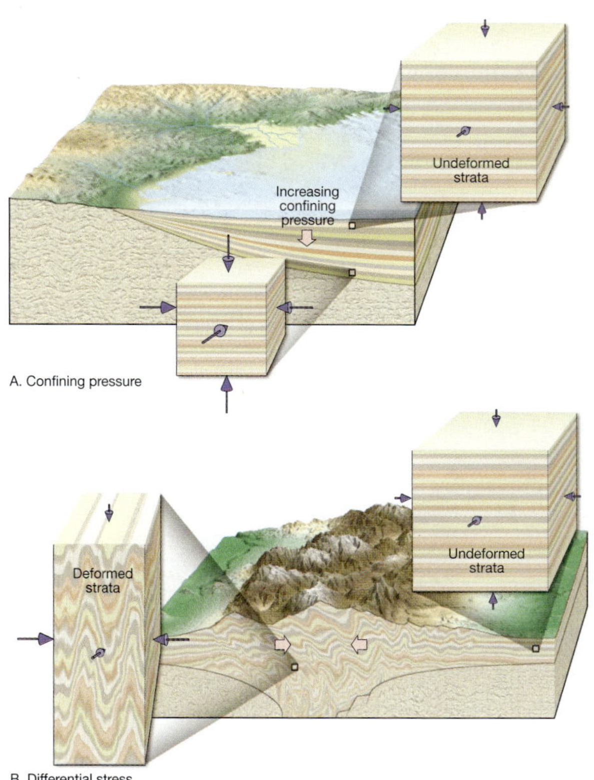

Figure 2.24 Pressure (stress) as a metamorphic agent.

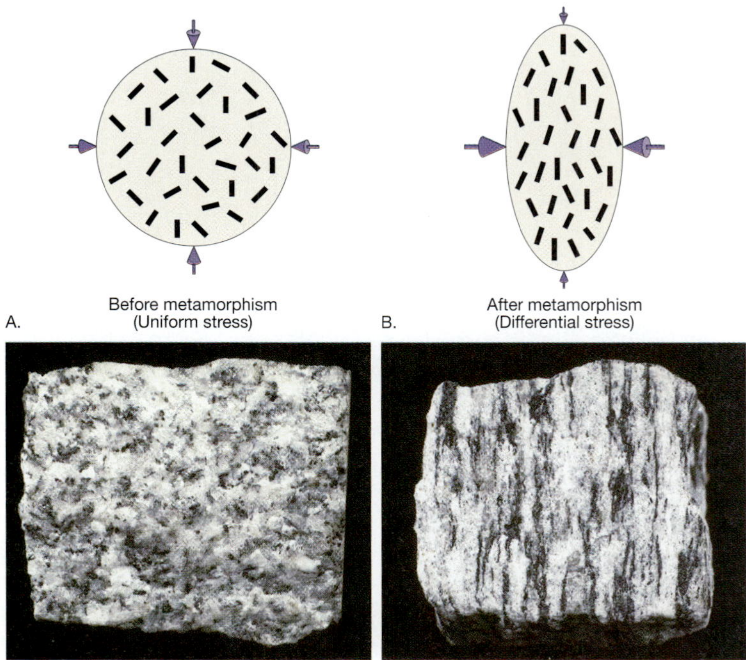

Figure 2.26 Mineral orientation before and after metamorphism.

Rock Name			Texture		Grain Size	Comments	Parent Rock
Slate	Increasing	Metamorphism	Foliated		Very fine	Excellent rock cleavage, smooth dull surfaces	Shale, mudstone, or siltstone
Phyllite					Fine	Breaks along wavey surfaces, glossy sheen	Slate
Schist					Medium to Coarse	Micaceous minerals dominate, scaly foliation	Phyllite
Gneiss					Medium to Coarse	Compositional banding due to segregation of minerals	Schist, granite, or volcanic rocks
Marble			Nonfoliated		Medium to coarse	Interlocking calcite or dolomite grains	Limestone, dolostone
Quartzite					Medium to coarse	Fused quartz grains, massive, very hard	Quartz sandstone
Anthracite					Fine	Shiny black organic rock that may exhibit conchoidal fracture	Bituminous coal

Figure 2.27 Classification of common metamorphic rocks.

NOTES:

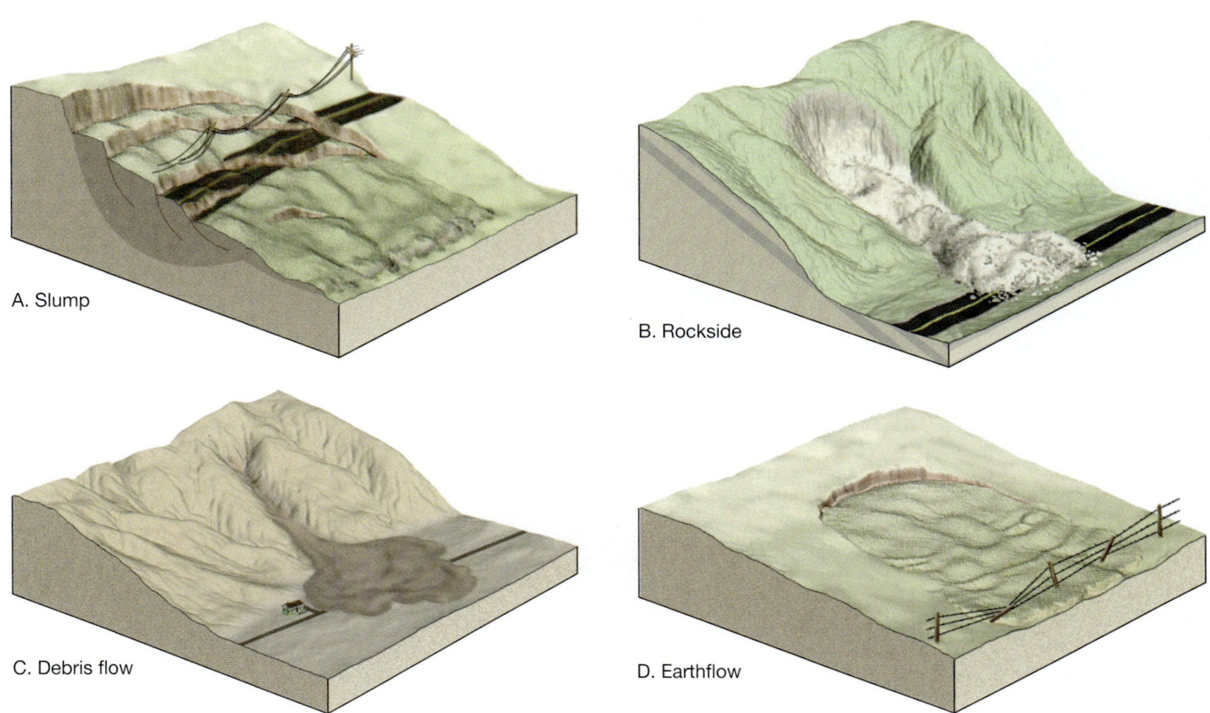

Figure 3.3 Four processes of mass wasting.

NOTES:

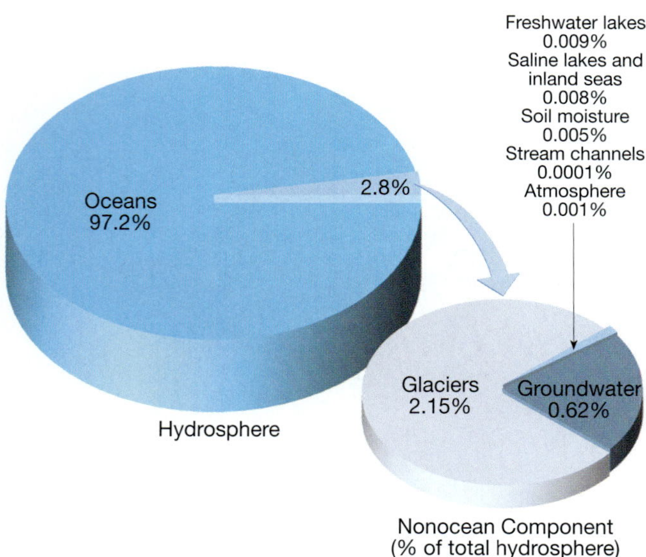

Figure 3.4 Distribution of Earth's water.

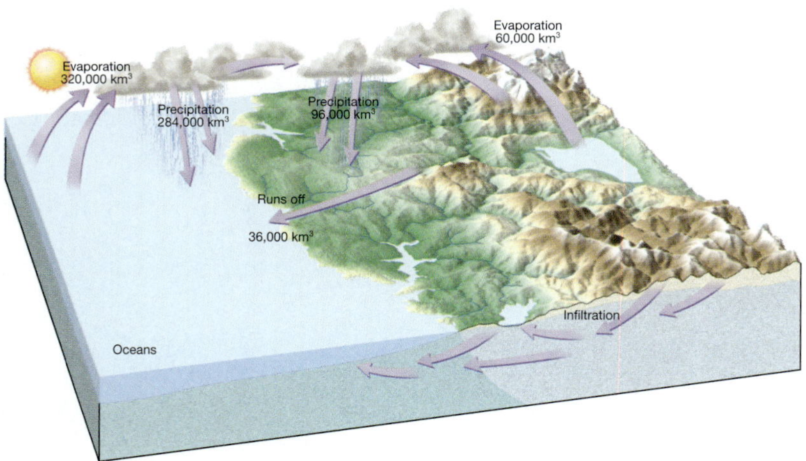

Figure 3.5 Earth's water balance.

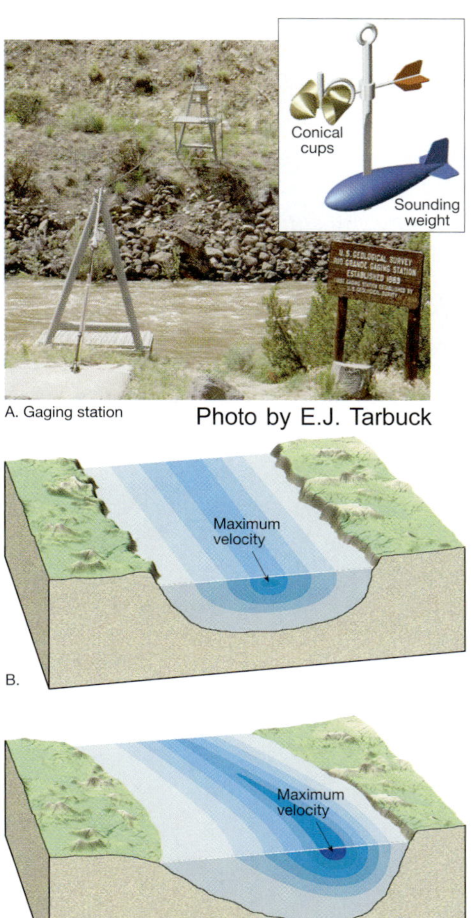

Figure 3.6 Velocity variation in straight and meandering streams.

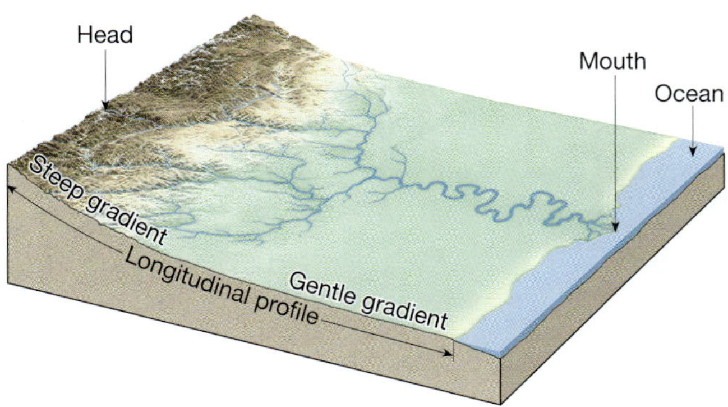

Figure 3.8 A longitudinal profile along the length of a stream.

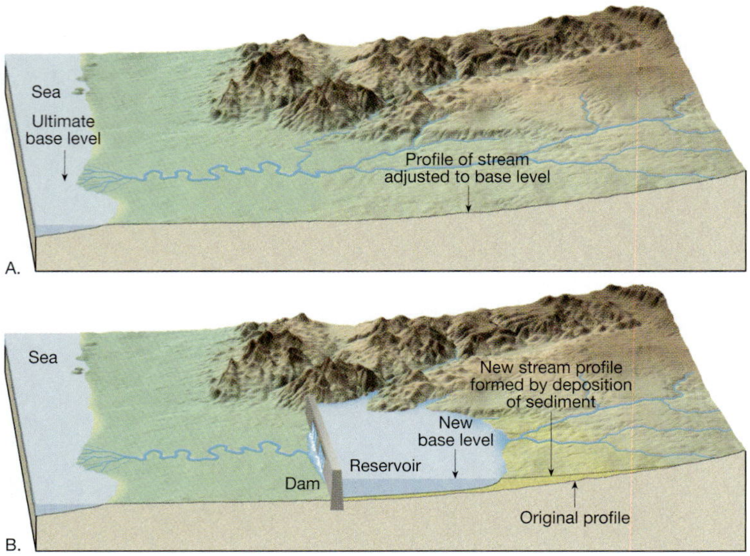

Figure 3.9 Stream adjustments when a dam is built.

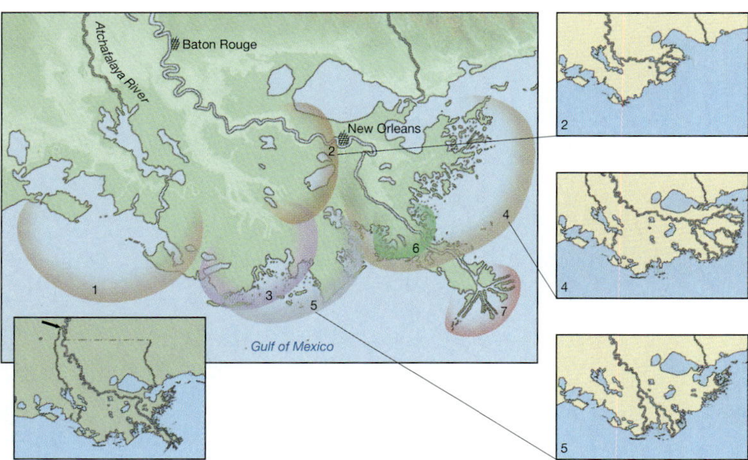

Figure 3.13 Mississippi delta.

NOTES:

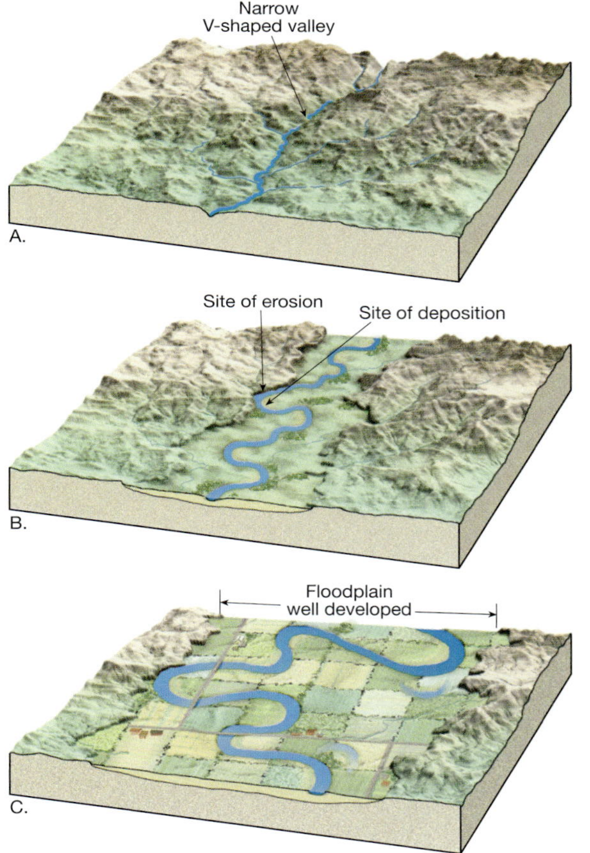

Figure 3.14 Natural levees.

Figure 3.16 Stream eroding its floodplain.

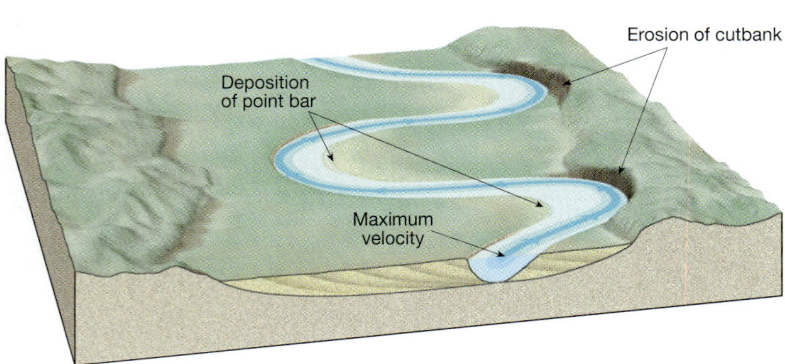

Figure 3.17 Lateral movement of meanders.

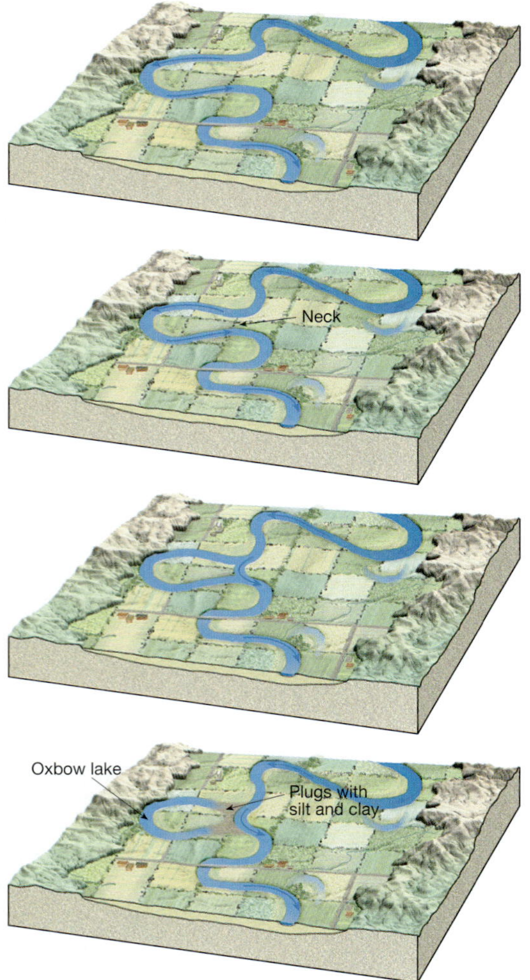

**Figure 3.18 Formation of a cutoff
and oxbow lake.**

Figure 3.21 The drainage basin of the Mississippi River.

NOTES:

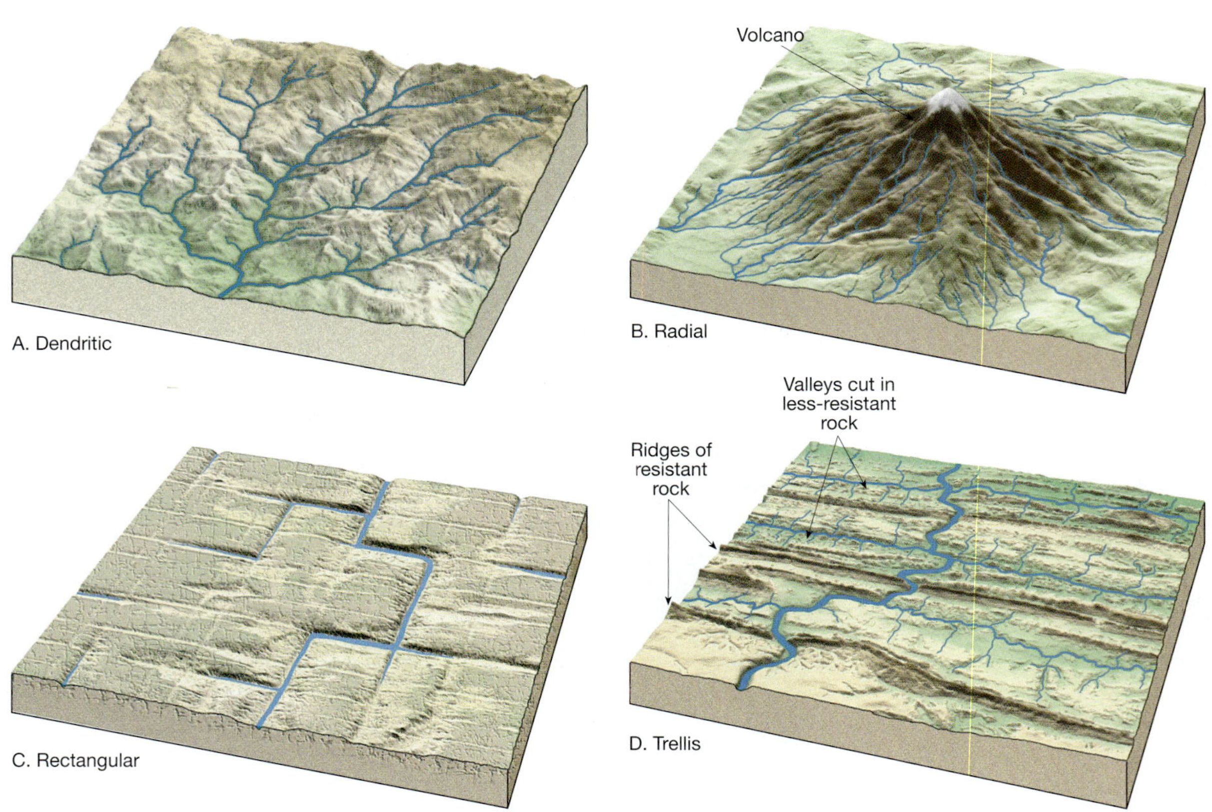

Figure 3.22 **Drainage patterns.**

NOTES:

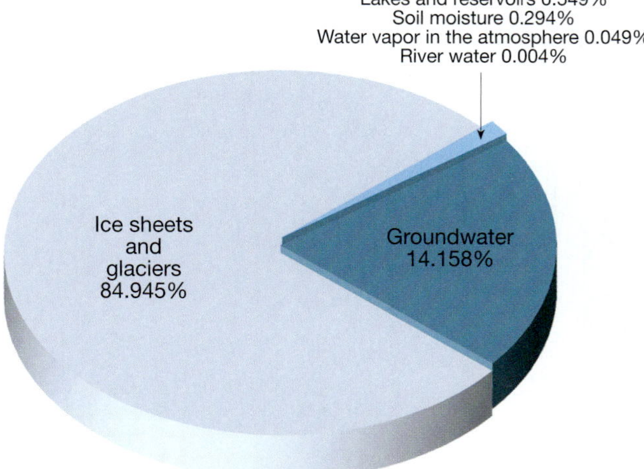

Figure 3.23 Distribution of fresh-water in the hydrosphere.

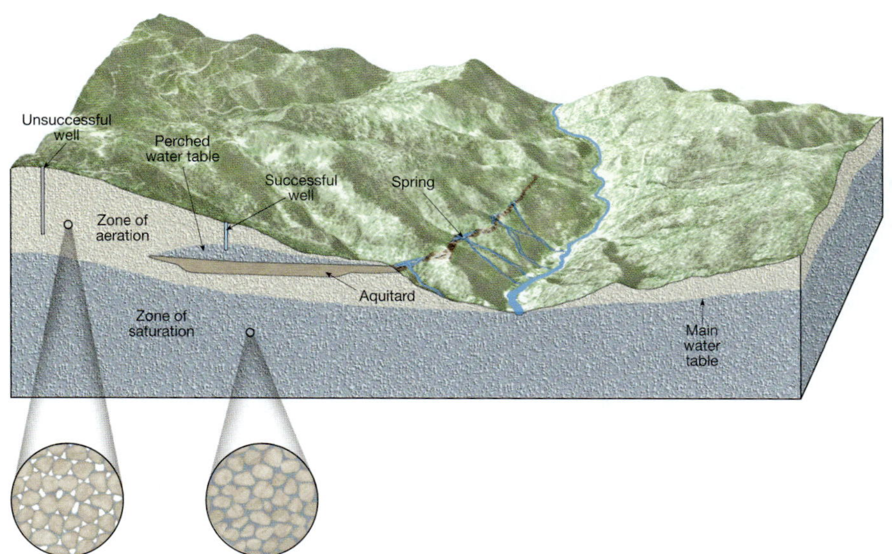

Figure 3.25 Features associated with subsurface water.

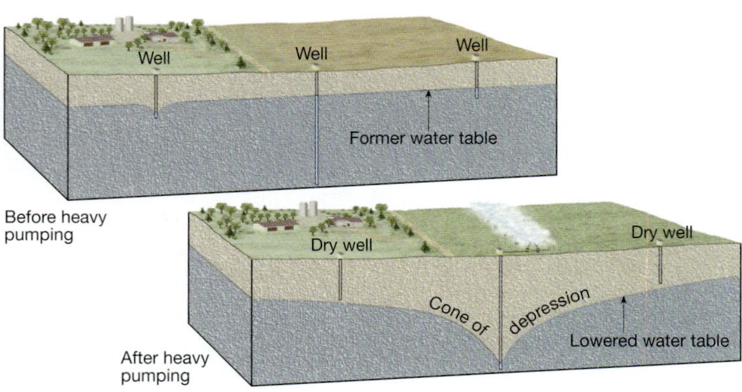

Figure 3.28 Cone of depression.

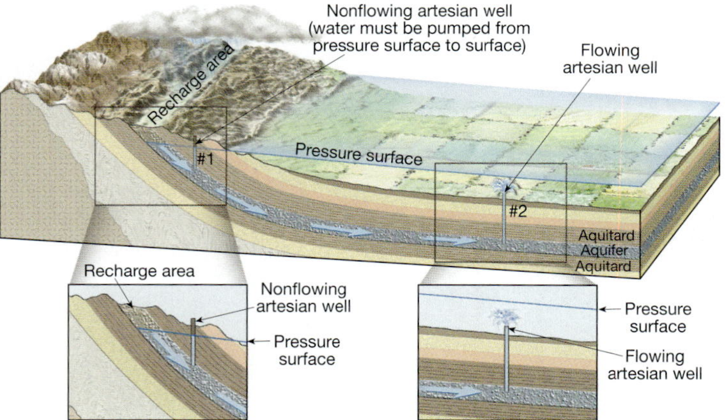

Figure 3.29 Artesian systems.

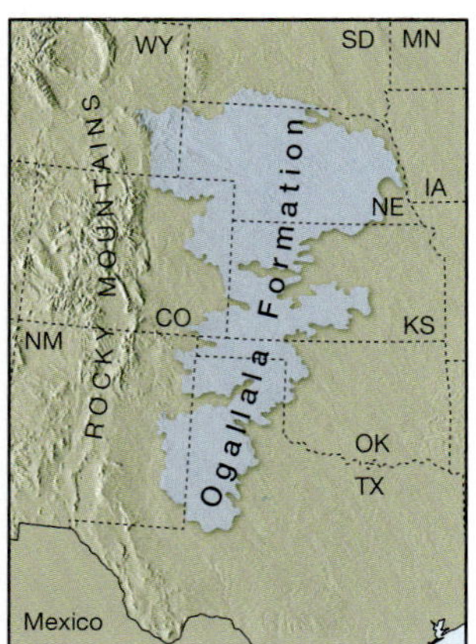

Figure 3.30 The Ogallala formation in the High Plains.

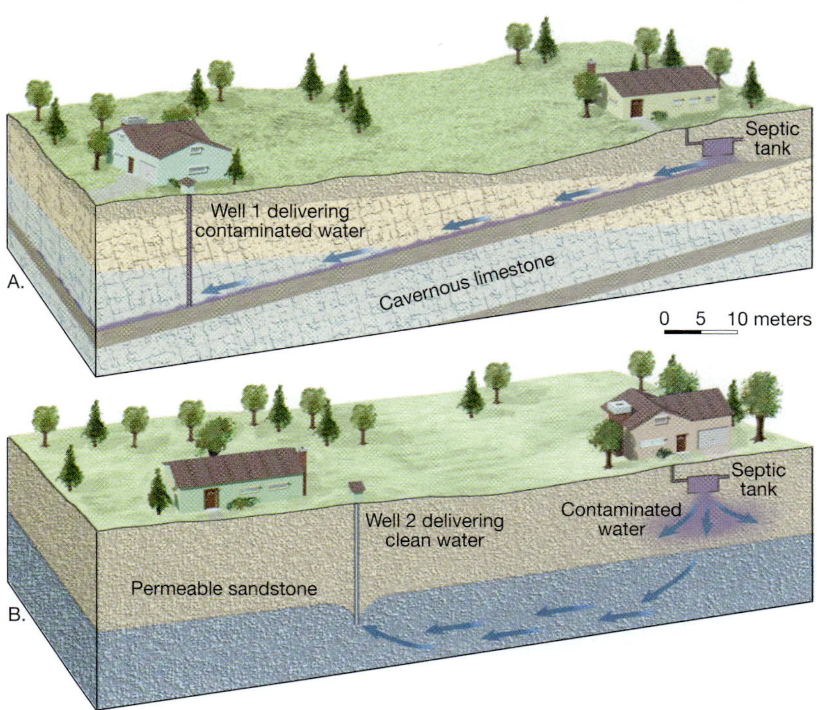

Figure 3.32 Aquifer permeability affects groundwater contamination.

NOTES:

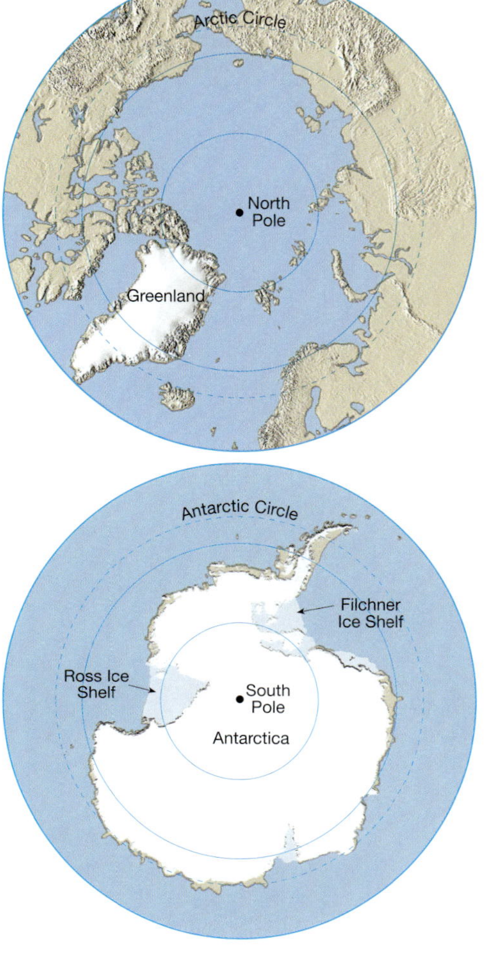

Figure 4.2 Greenland and Antarctica.

Figure 4.3 The zone of accumulation and the zone of wastage.

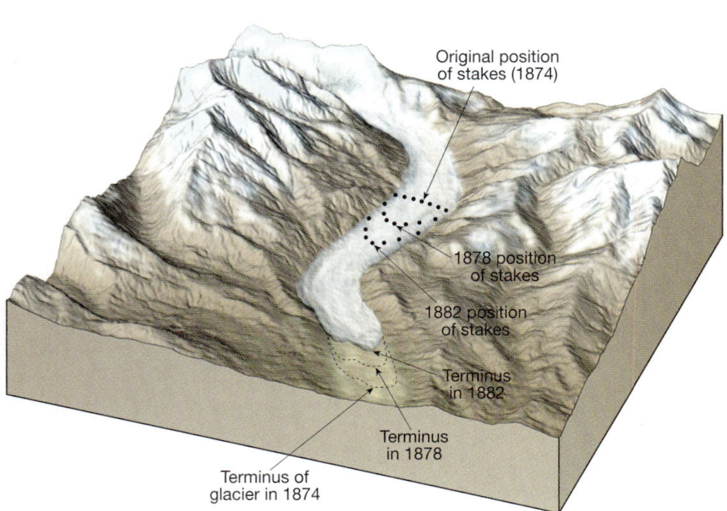

Figure 4.4 Ice movement and changes in the terminus at Rhone Glacier.

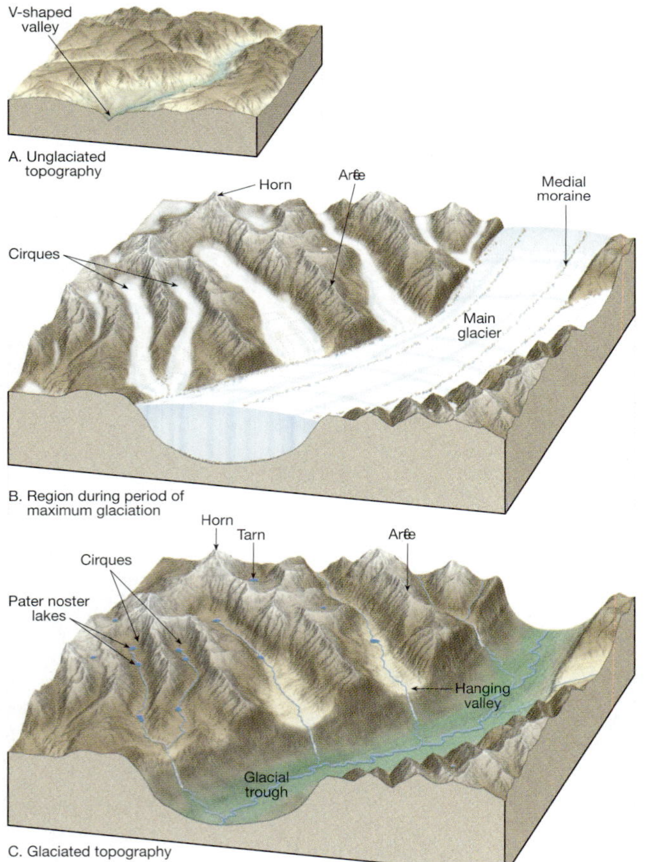

Figure 4.7 The development of erosional landforms created by alpine glaciers.

NOTES:

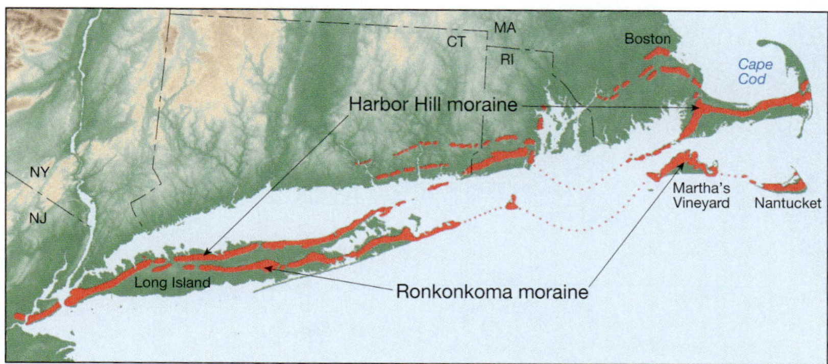

Figure 4.13 End moraines along Long Island, Cape Cod, Martha's Vineyard, and Nantucket.

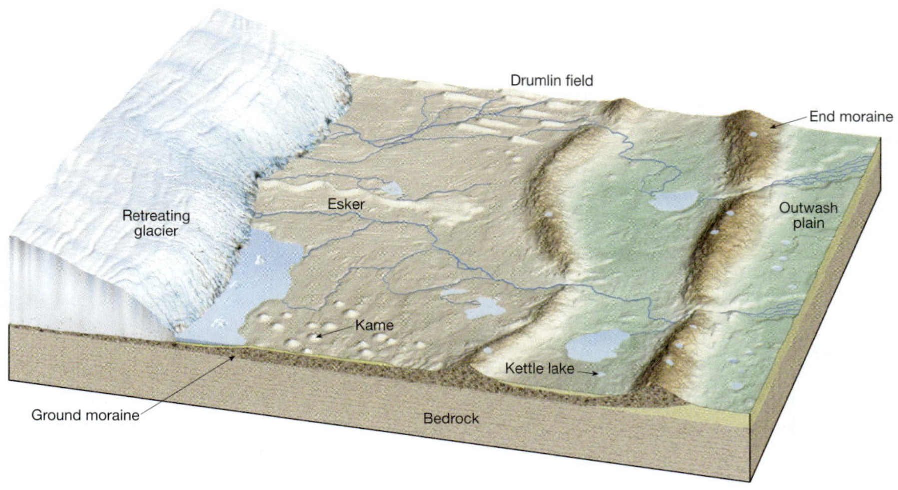

Figure 4.14 Common depositional landforms.

Figure 4.15 Maximum extent of glaciation in the Northern Hemisphere during the Ice Age.

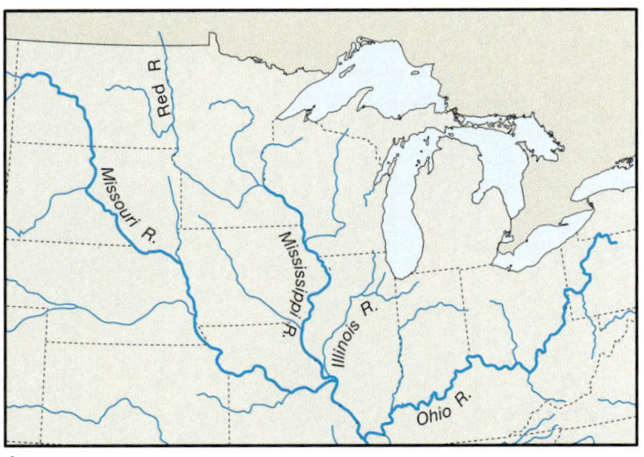

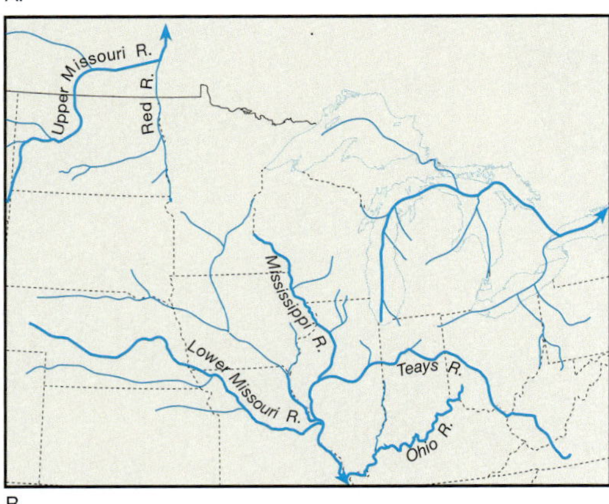

Figure 4.16 Present-day pattern of rivers in the central United States and reconstruction of drainage systems prior to the Ice Age.

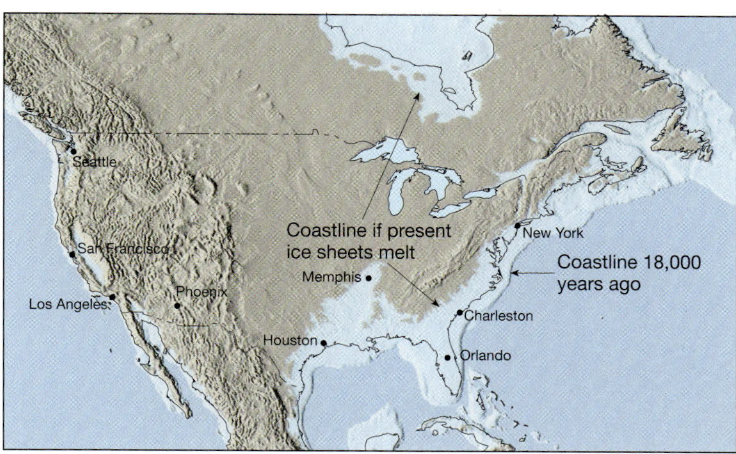

Figure 4.17 Present-day coastline compared to the coastline during the last ice-age maximum and the coastline if present ice sheets melted.

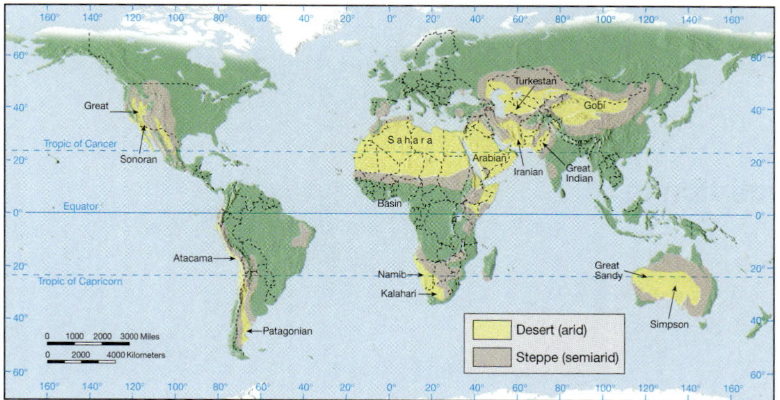

Figure 4.19 Arid and semiarid climates of Earth's land surface.

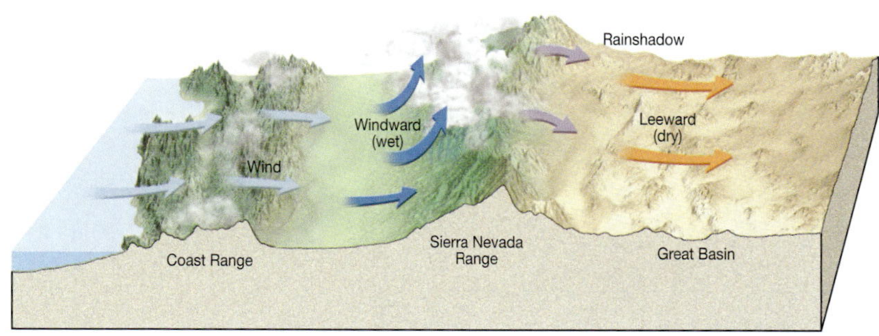

Figure 4.21 Rainshadow desert.

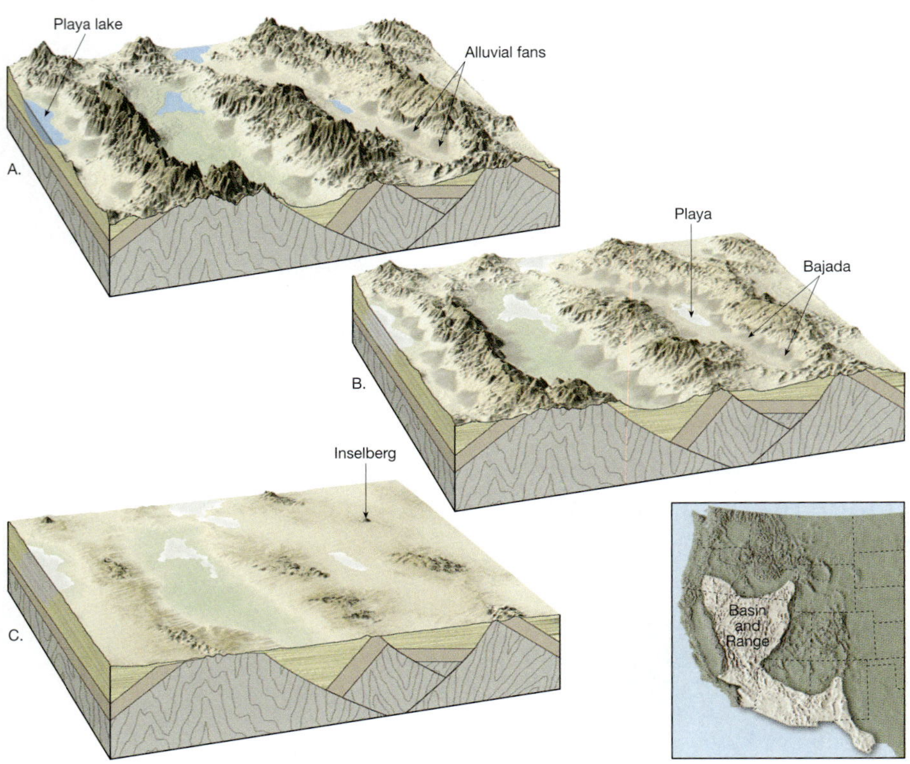

Figure 4.23 Stages of landscape evolution in a mountainous desert.

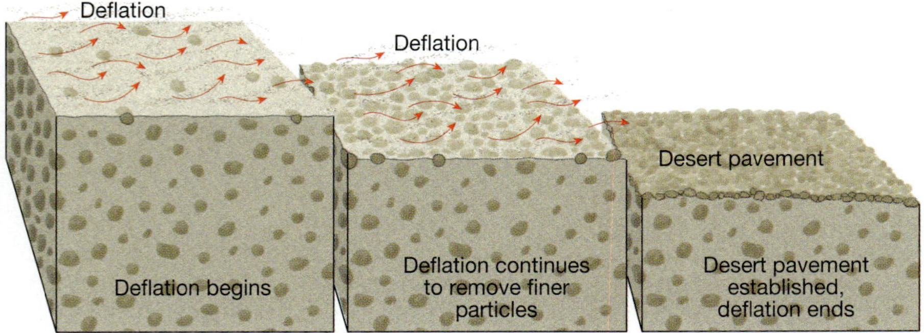

Figure 4.27 A Formation of desert pavement.

CHAPTER 5 - Plate Tectonics: A Scientific Theory Unfolds

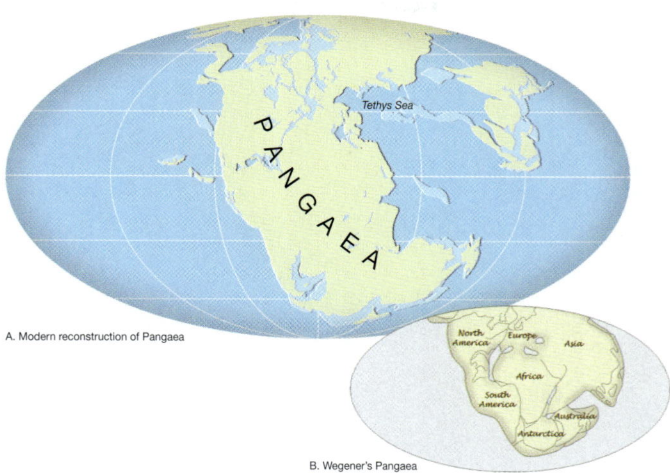

Figure 5.2 Reconstruction of Pangaea.

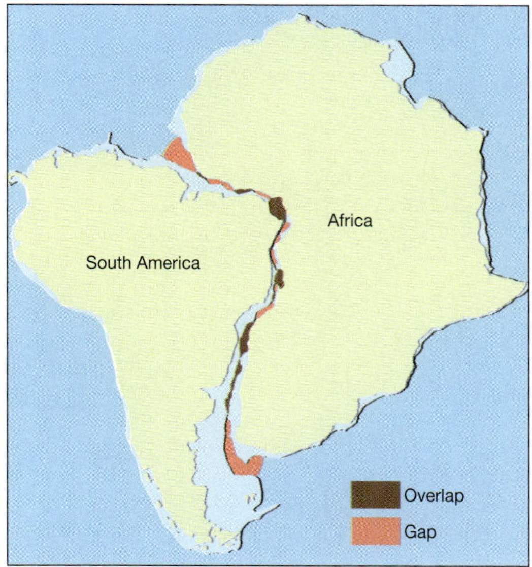

Figure 5.3 The best fit of South America and Africa along the continental slope.

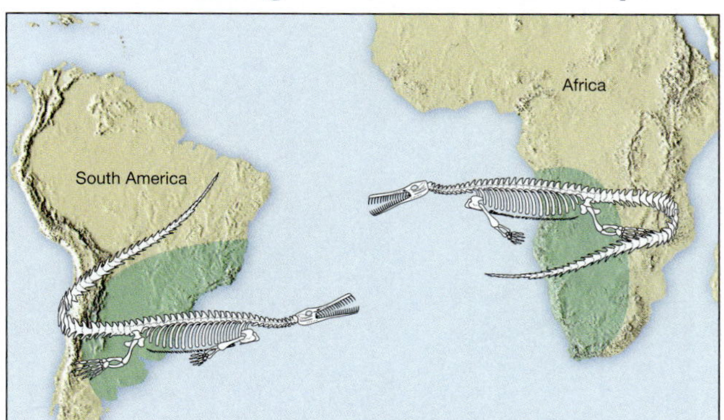

Figure 5.4 Distribution of *Mesosaurus.*

Figure 5.5 Matching mountain ranges across the North Atlantic.

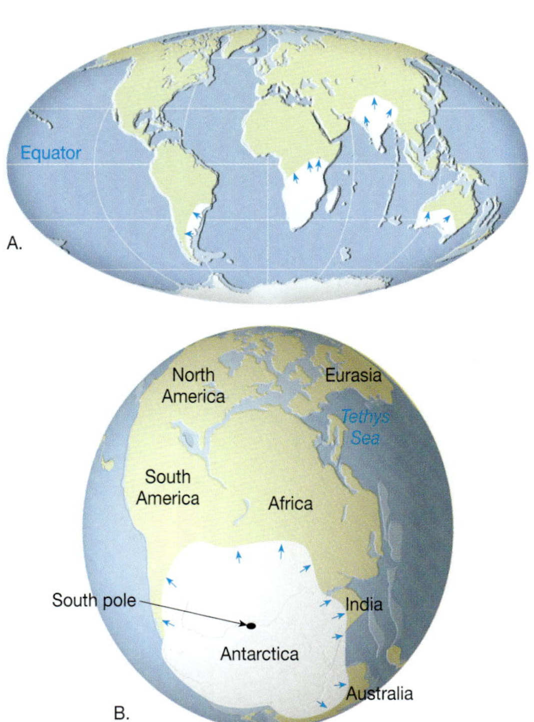

Figure 5.6 Paleoclimatic evidence for continental drift.

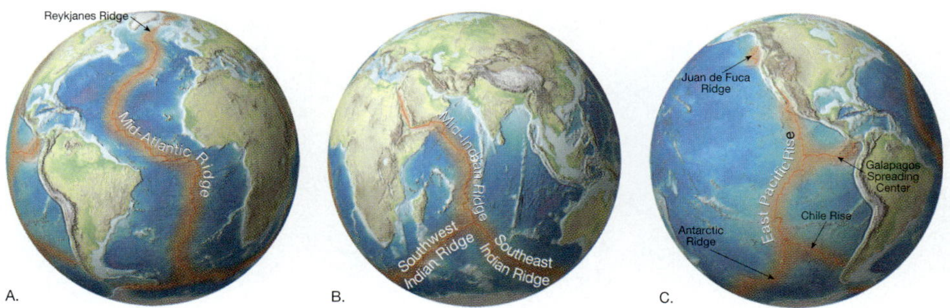

Figure 5.7 Distribution of the oceanic ridge sytem.

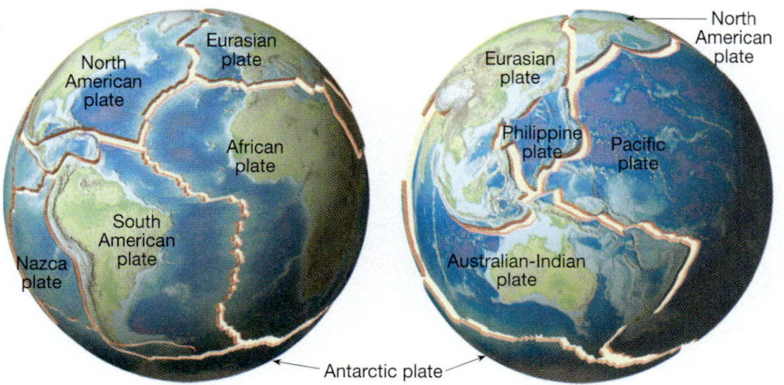

Figure 5.8 Illustration of some of Earth's lithospheric plates.

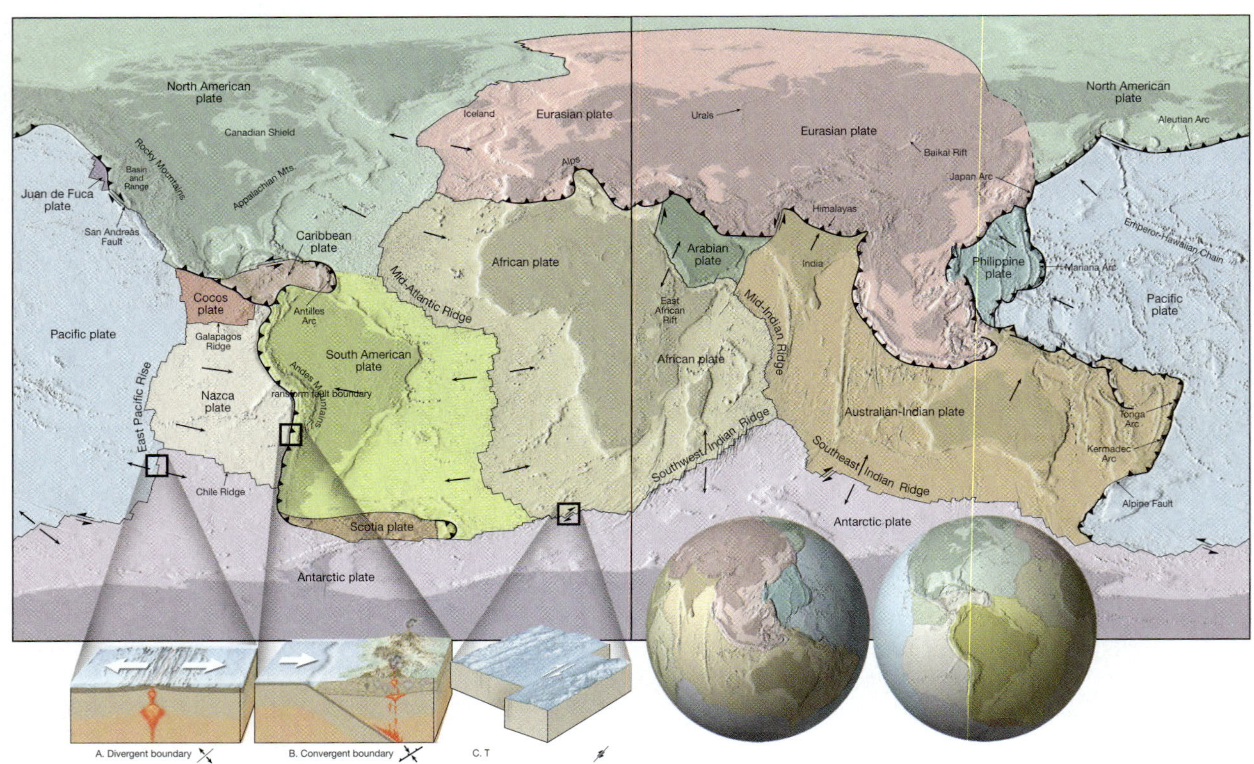

Figure 5.9 A mosaic of rigid plates constitutes Earth's outer shell.

NOTES:

NOTES:

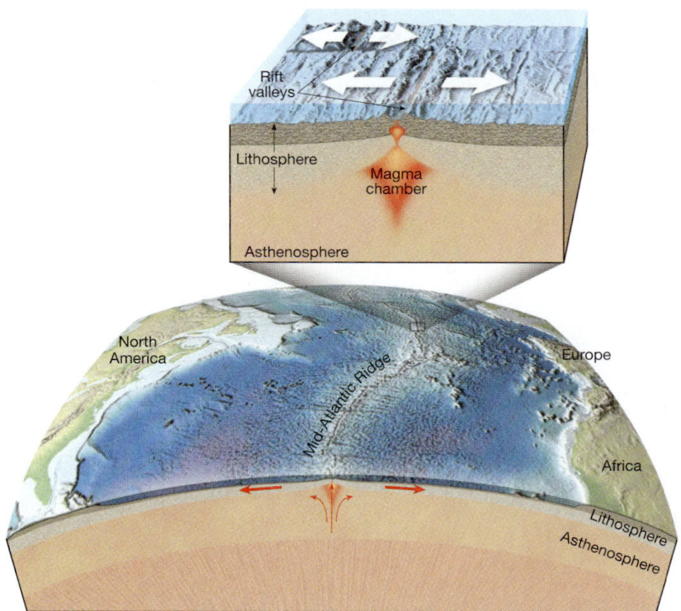

Figure 5.10 Divergent plate boundaries.

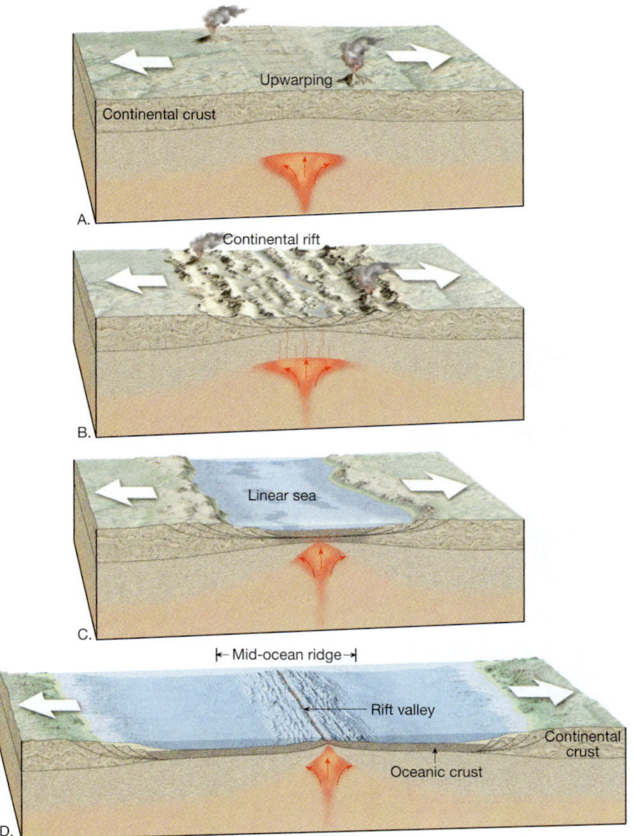

Figure 5.11 Continental rifting and the formation of a new ocean basin.

NOTES:

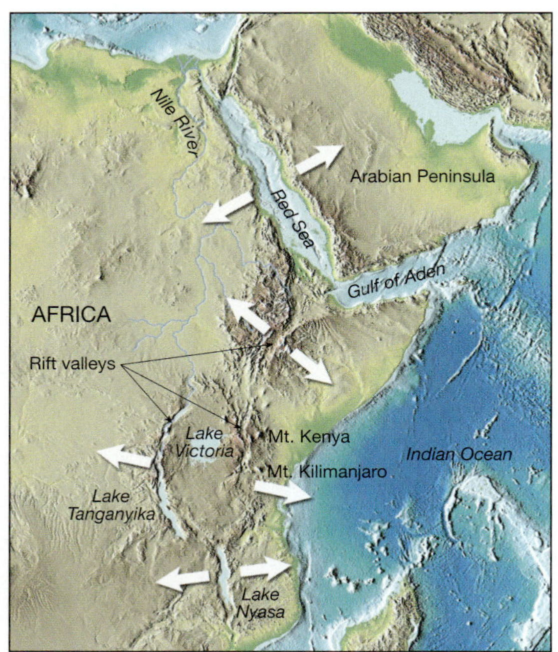

Figure 5.12 **East African rift valleys.**

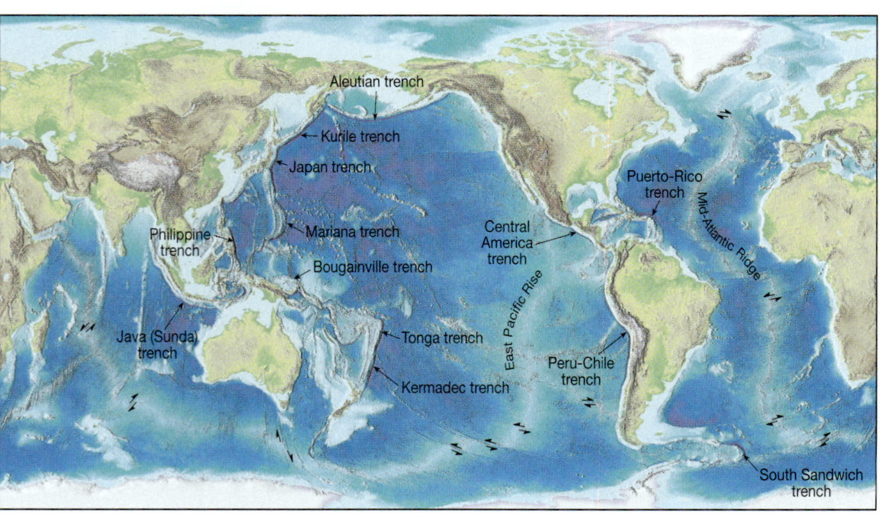

Figure 5.13 **Distribution of the world's oceanic trenches, ridge system, and transform faults.**

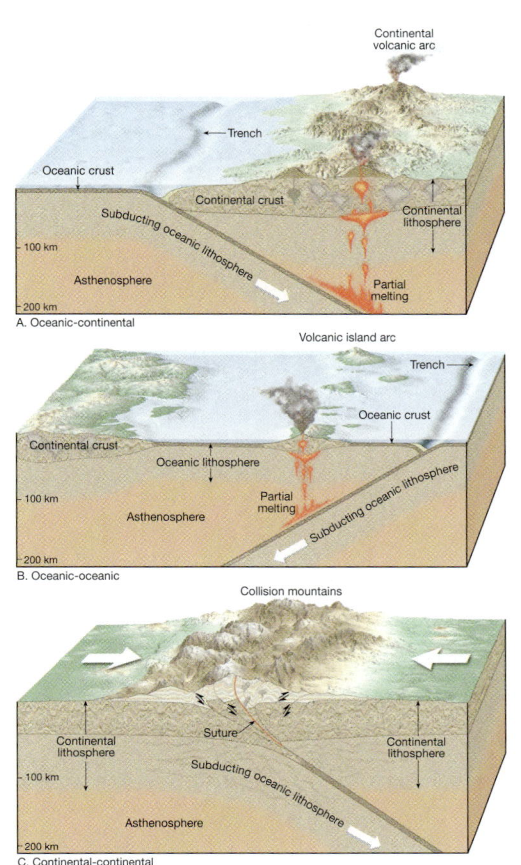

Figure 5.14 Three types of convergent plate boundaries.

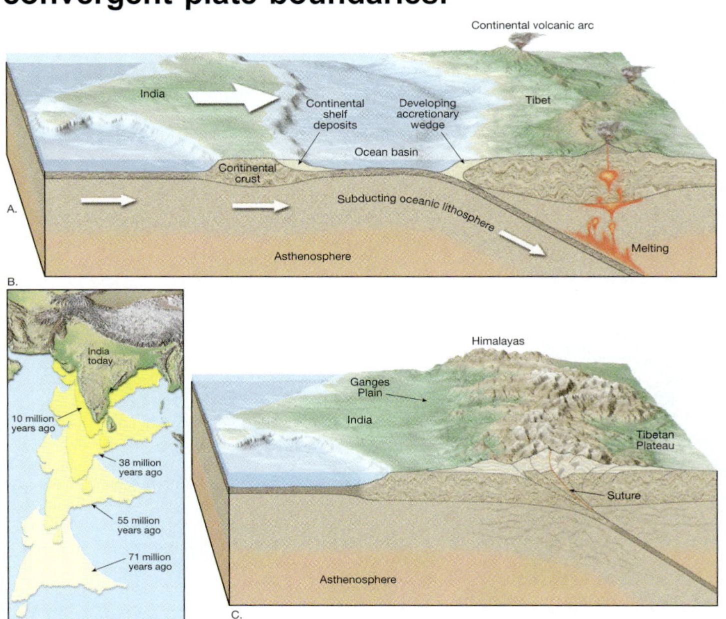

Figure 5.15 The ongoing collision of India and Asia.

NOTES:

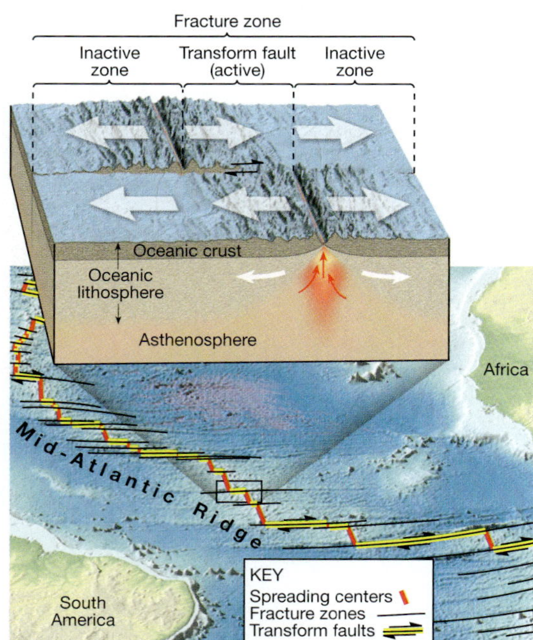

Figure 5.16 **A transform fault joining segments of the Mid-Atlantic Ridge.**

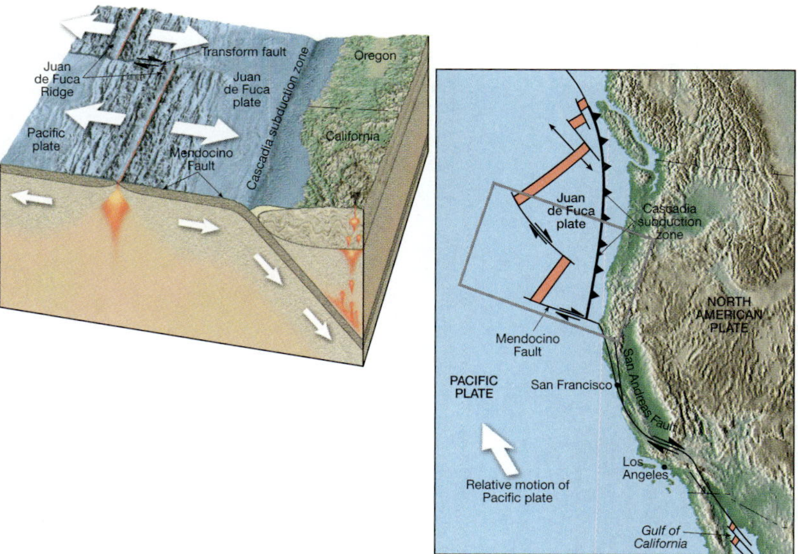

Figure 5.17 **The Mendocino transform fault.**

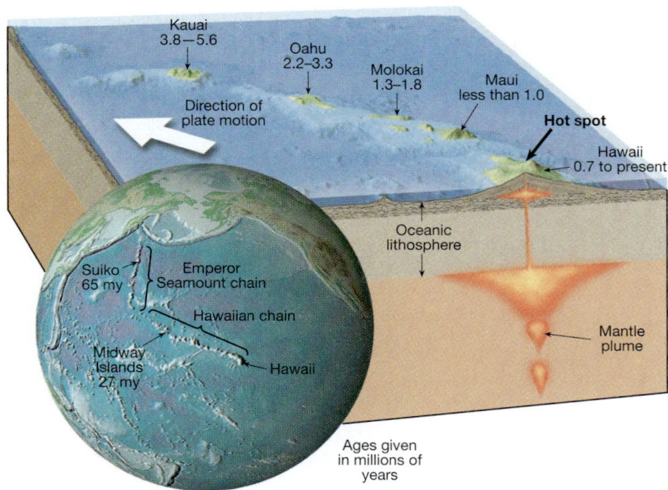

Figure 5.19 Hawaiian Islands-Emperor seamount chain.

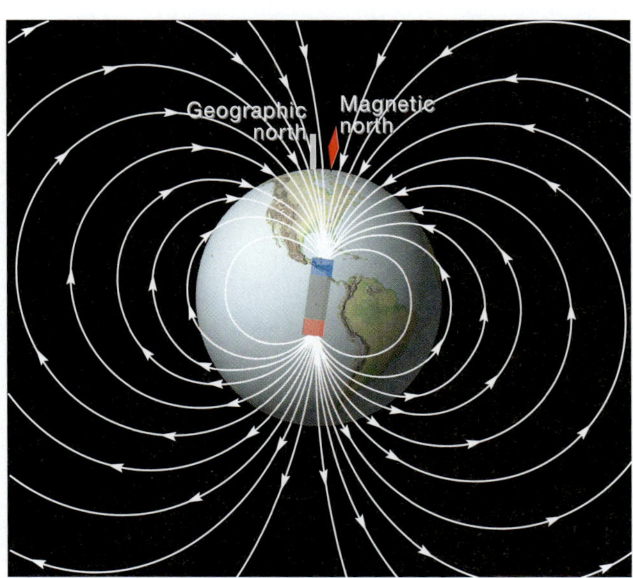

Figure 5.20 Earth's magnetic field.

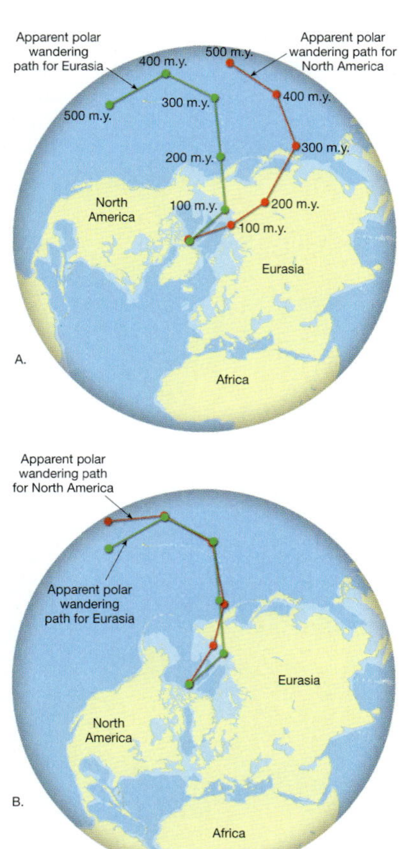

Figure 5.21 Simplified apparent polar wandering paths.

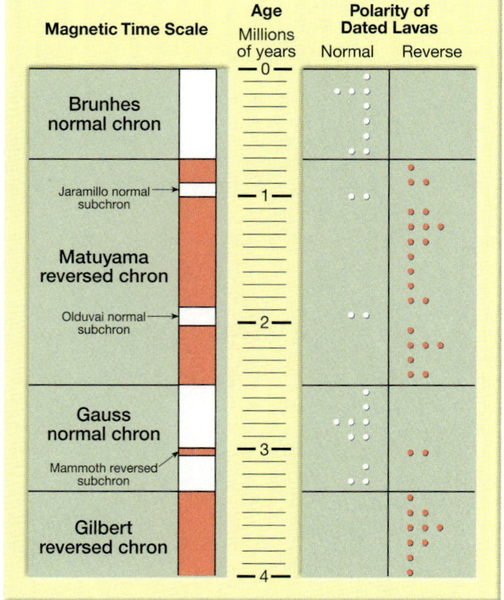

Figure 5.22 Time scale of Earth's magnetic field in the recent past.

NOTES:

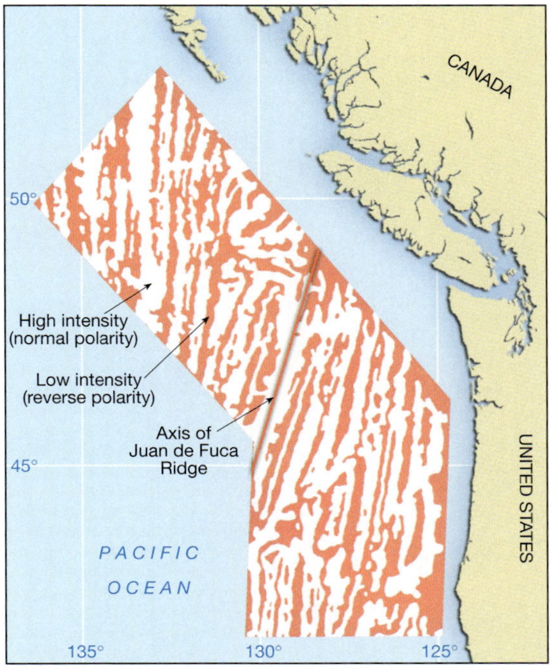

Figure 5.23 Stripes of high- and low-intensity magnetism off the Pacific Coast of North America.

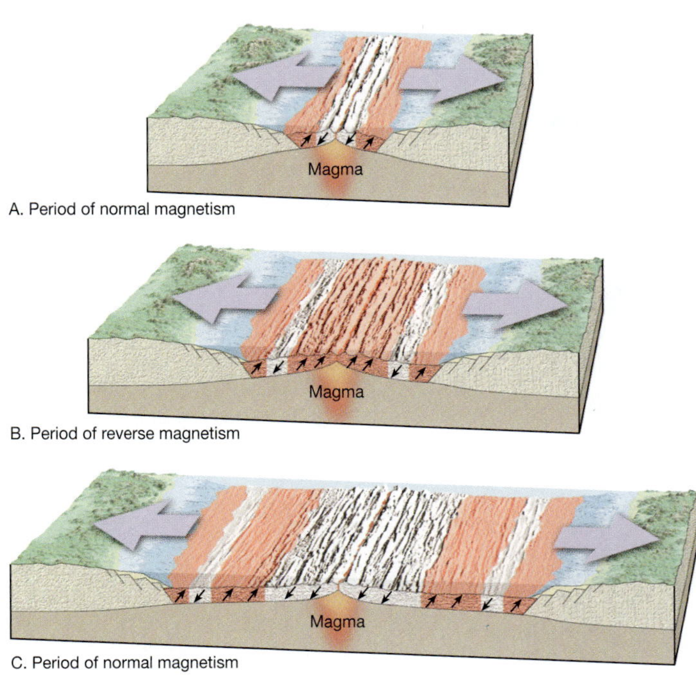

Figure 5.24 The mid-ocean ridge and magnetic reversals.

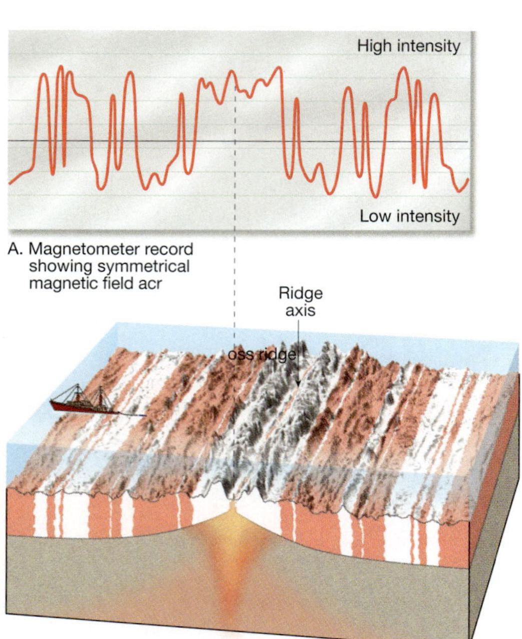

Figure 5.25 **The ocean floor as a magnetic tape recorder.**

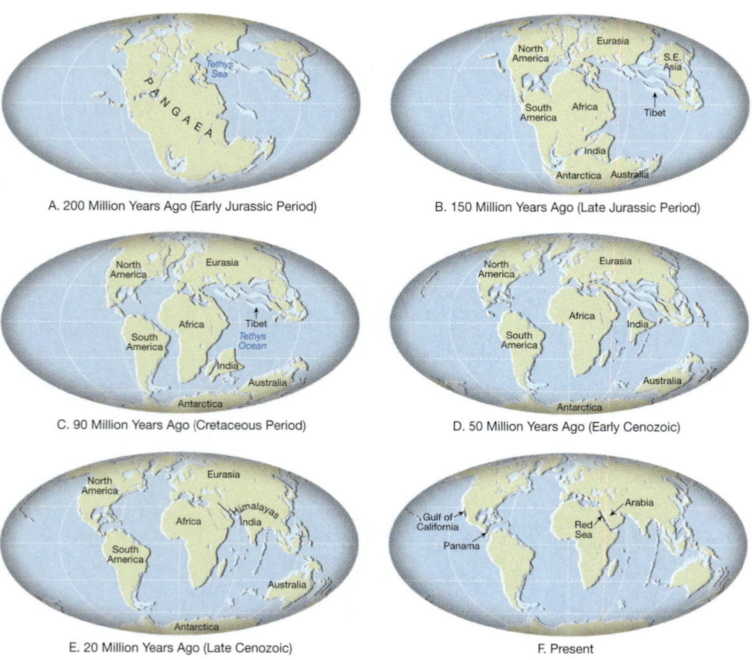

Figure 5.26 **Several views of the breakup of Pangaea.**

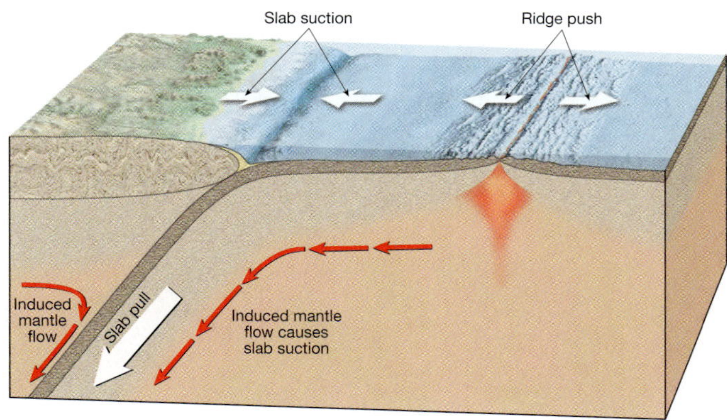

Figure 5.27 Some of the forces that act on plates.

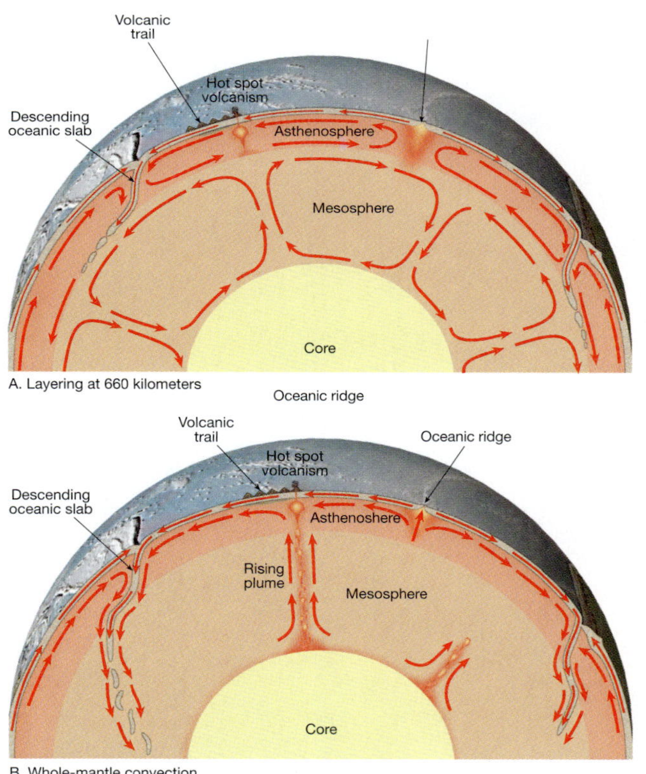

Figure 5.28 Proposed models for mantle convection.

CHAPTER 6 - Restless Earth: Earthquakes, Geologic Structures, and Mountain Building

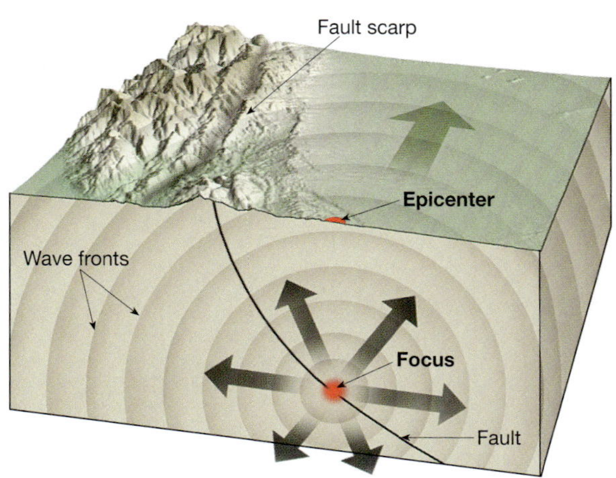

Figure 6.2 The focus of an earthquake.

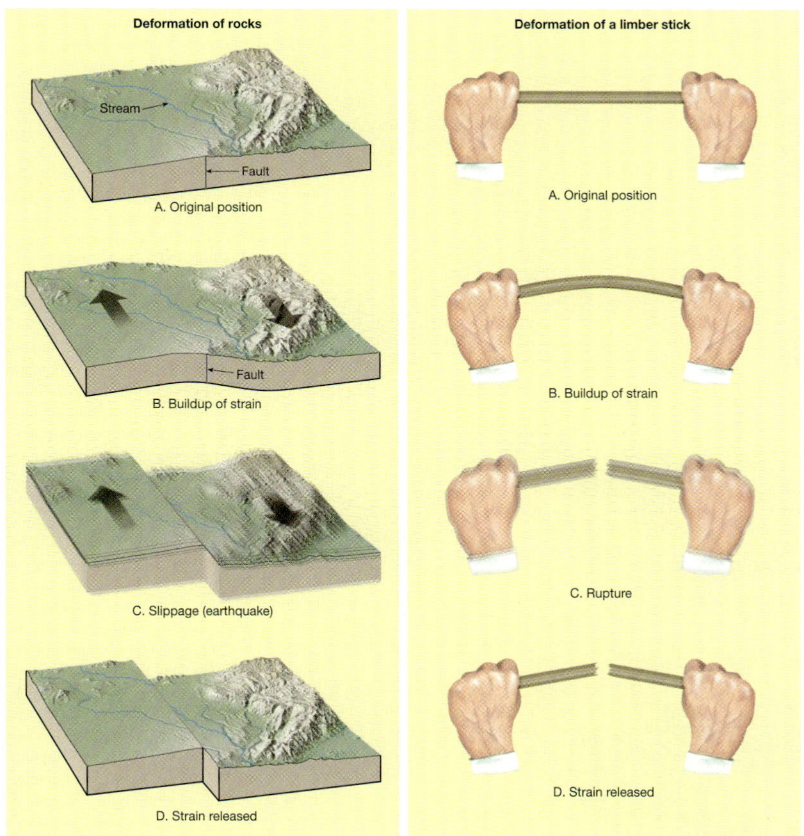

Figure 6.5 Elastic rebound.

NOTES:

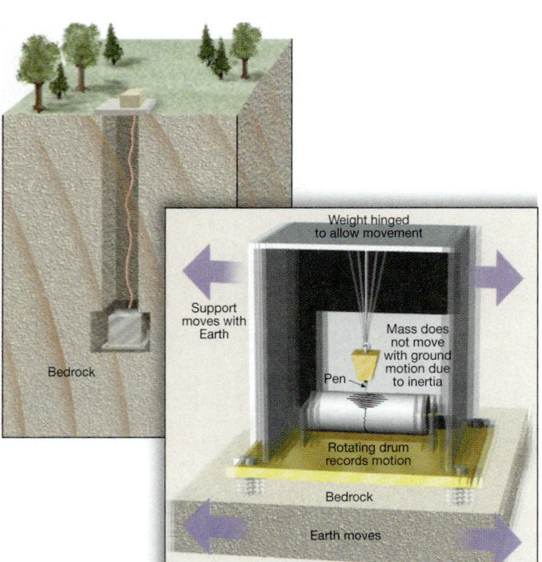

Figure 6.6 **Principle of the seismograph.**

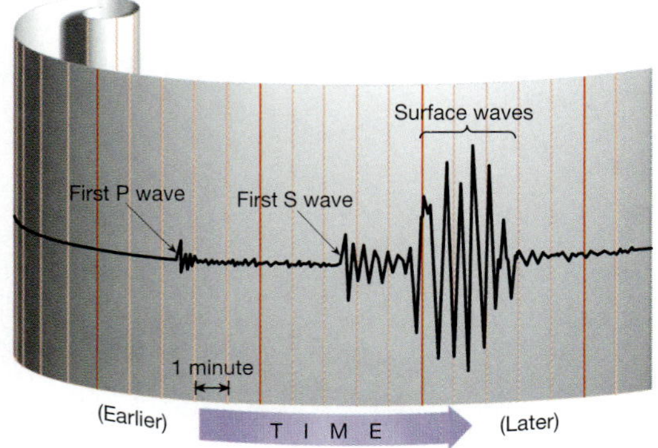

Figure 6.7 **Typical seismic record.**

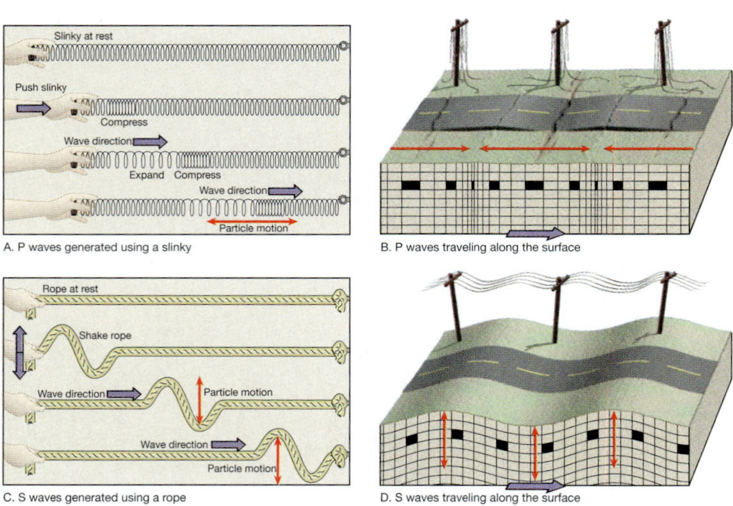

Figure 6.8 **Types of seismic waves and their characteristic motion.**

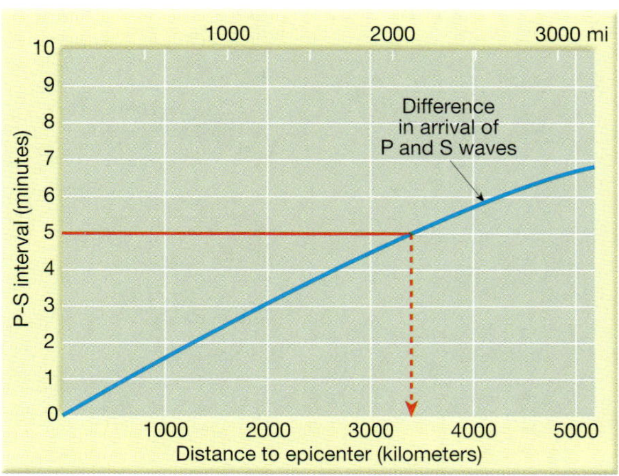

Figure 6.9 A travel-time graph.

Figure 6.2 Locating an earthquake epicenter.

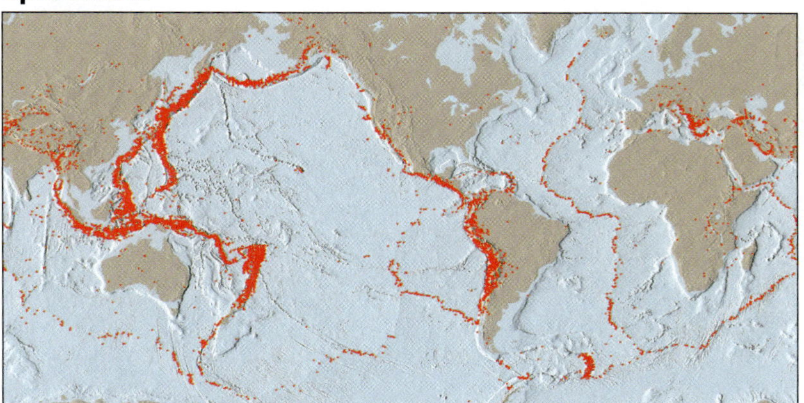

Figure 6.11 Distribution of earthquakes.

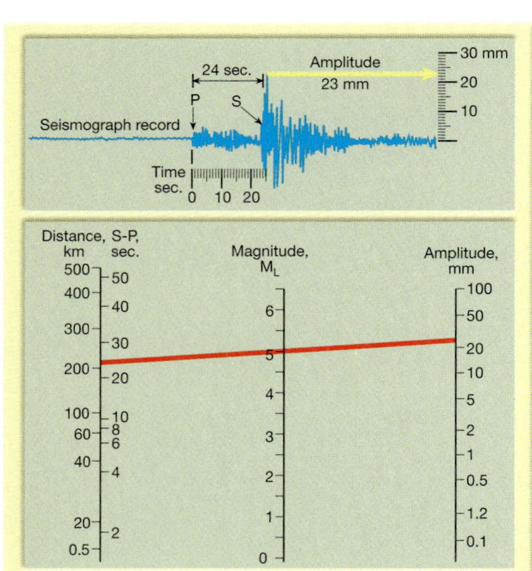

Figure 6.12 Determining Richter magnitude.

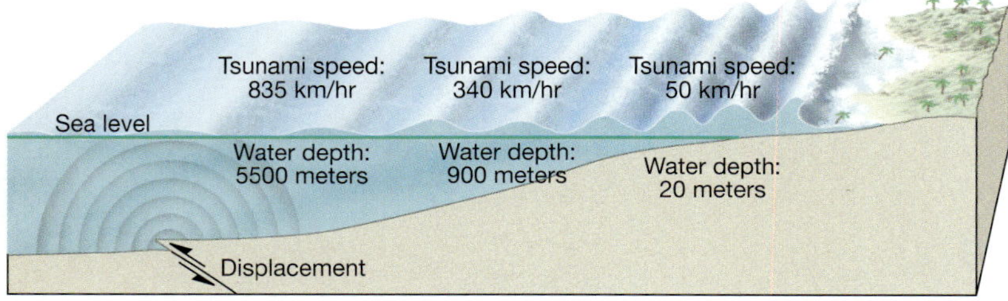

Figure 6.15 Tsunami.

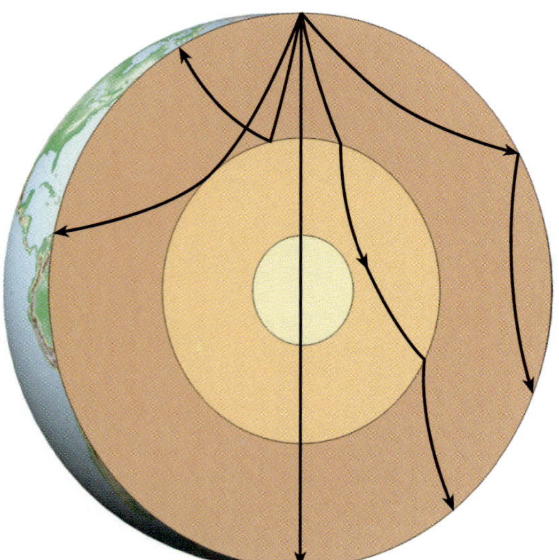

Figure 6.17 Possible paths that seismic rays take through Earth.

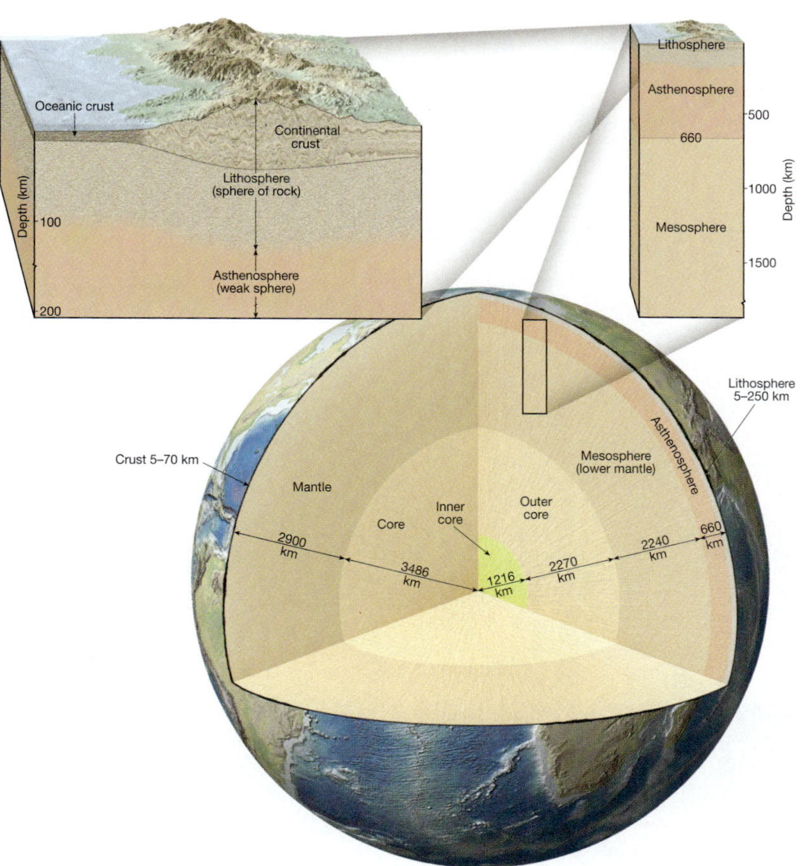

Figure 6.18 **Views of Earth's layered structure.**

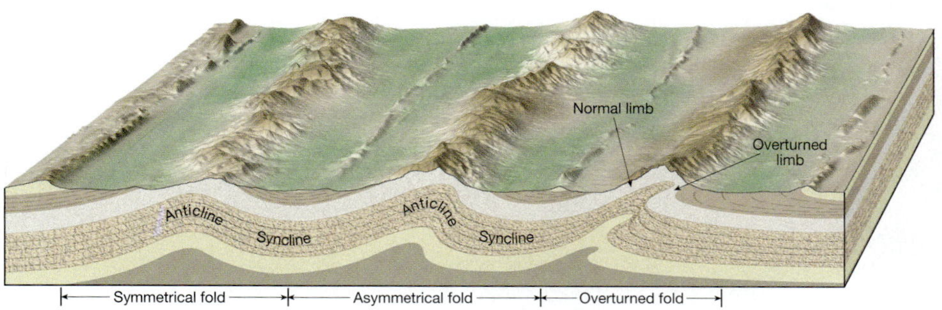

Figure 6.20 **Block diagram of principle types of folded strata.**

NOTES:

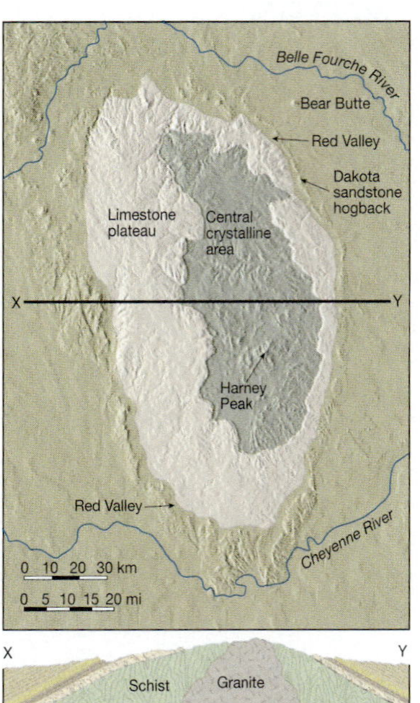

Figure 6.21 The Black Hills of South Dakota.

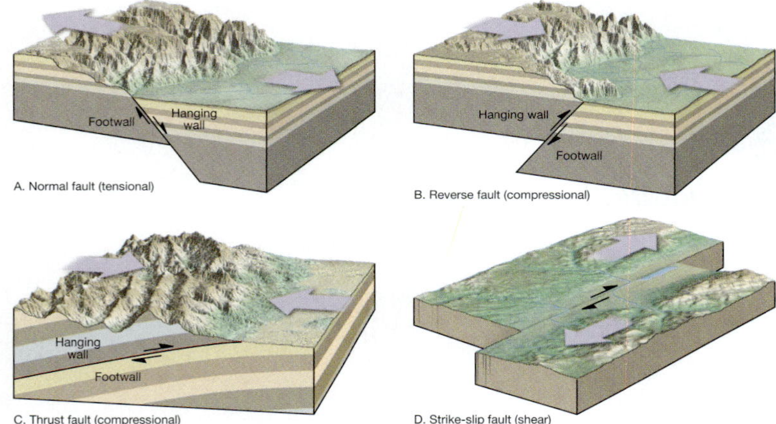

Figure 6.24 Four types of faults.

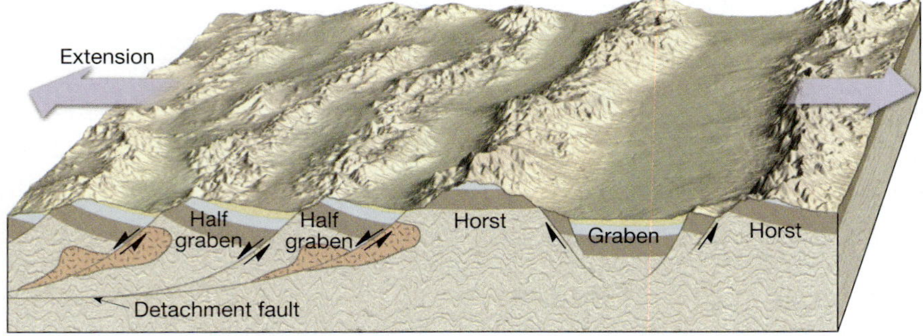

Figure 6.25 Normal faulting in the Basin and Range Province.

Figure 6.26 **Map showing the extent of the San Andreas fault system.**

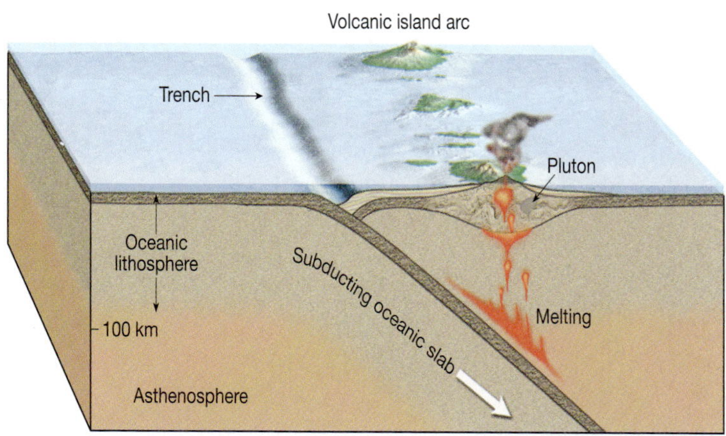

Figure 6.28 **Development of a volcanic island arc.**

NOTES:

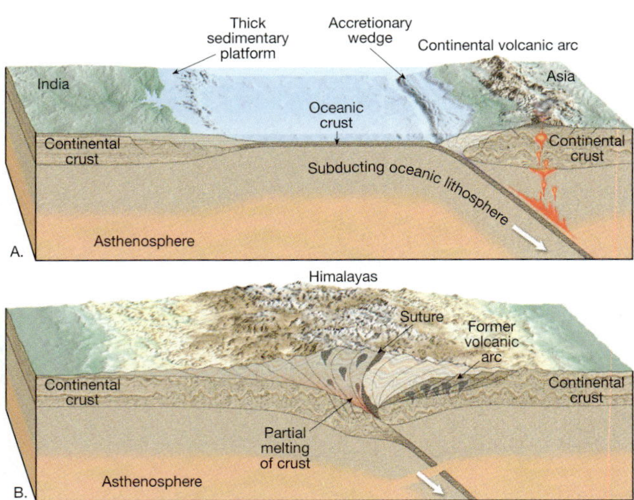

Figure 6.29 **Orogenesis along an Andean-type subduction zone.**

Figure 6.30 **Collision of India with the Eurasian plate.**

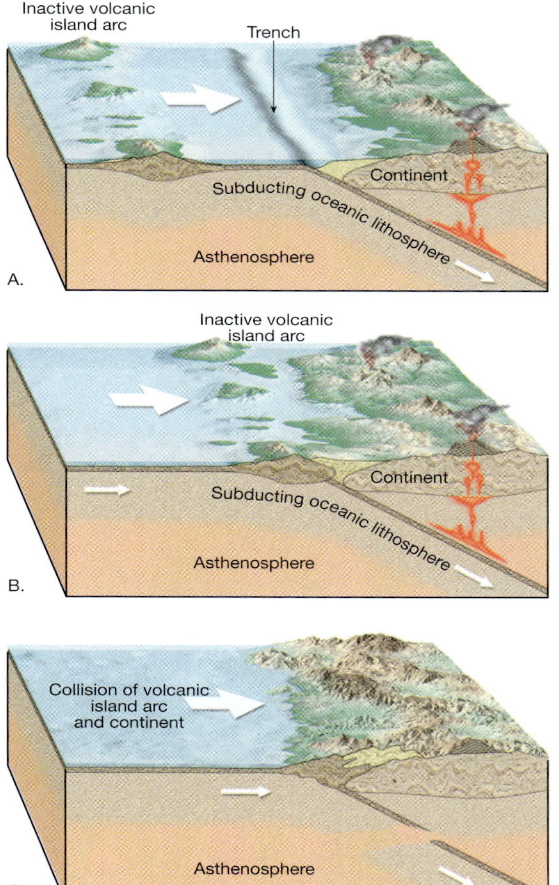

Figure 6.31 Distribution of present-day oceanic plateaus.

Figure 6.32 The collision and accretion of an island arc to a continental margin.

NOTES:

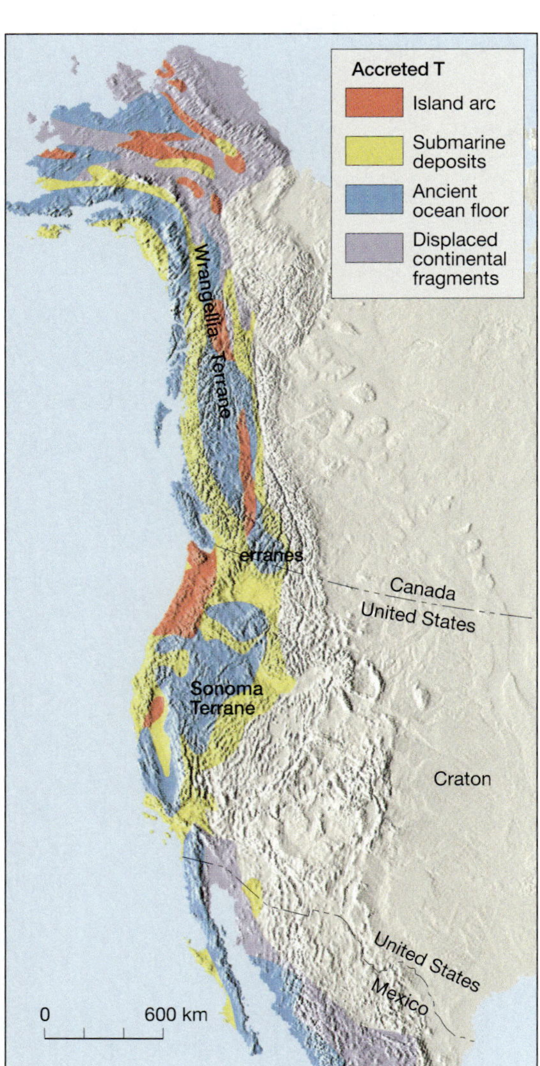

Figure 6.33 Terranes thought to have been added to western North America during the past 200 million years.

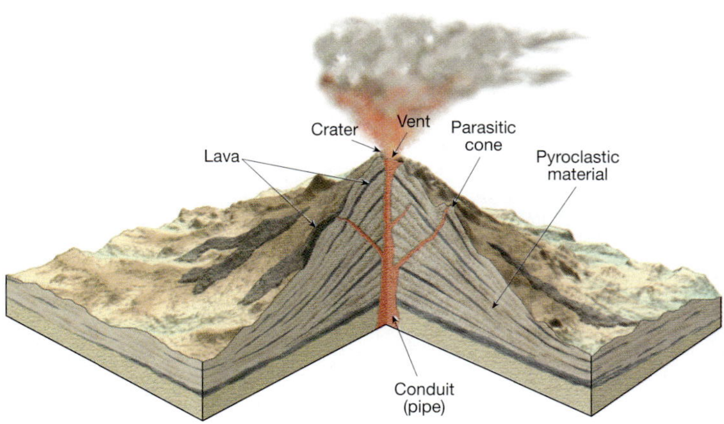

Figure 7.7 Anatomy of a "typical" composite cone.

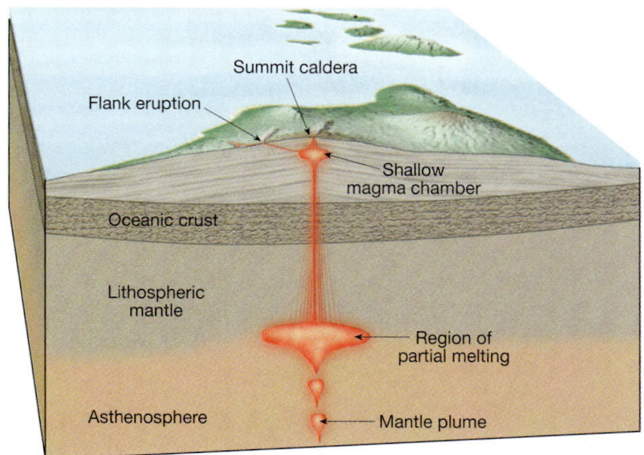

Figure 7.8 Mauna Loa is a shield volcano.

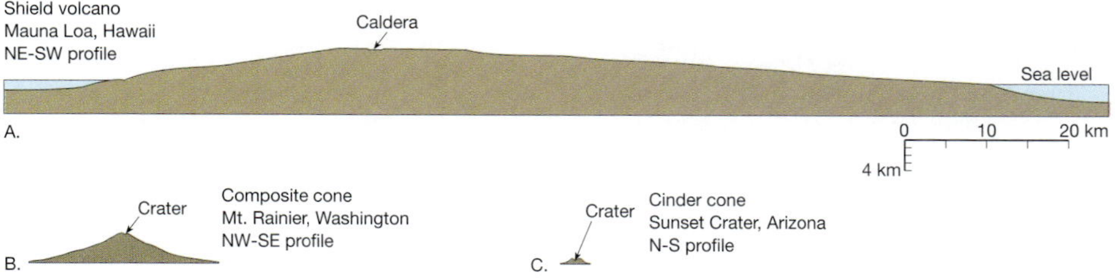

Figure 7.9 Profiles of volcanoes.

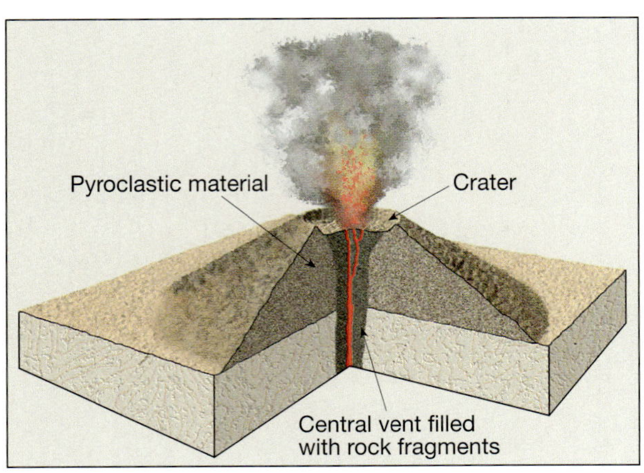

Figure 7.11 Cinder cone.

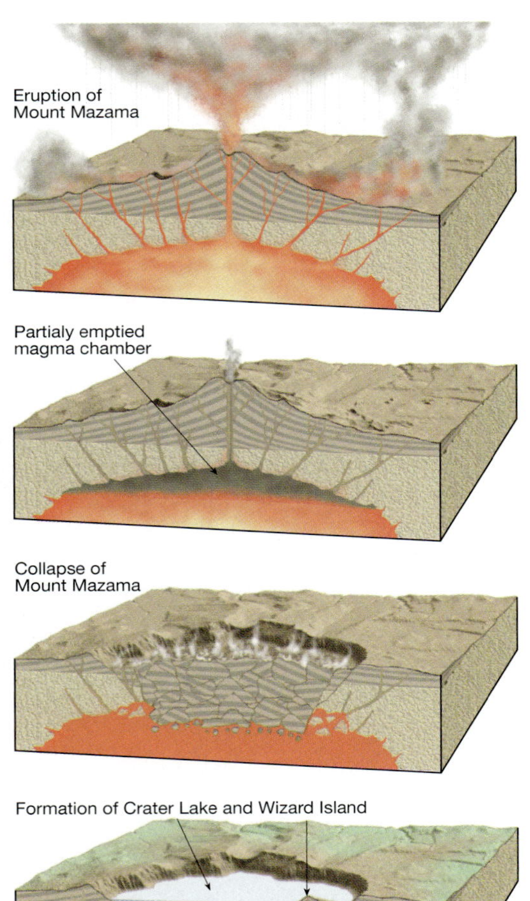

Figure 7.17 Formation of Crater Lake.

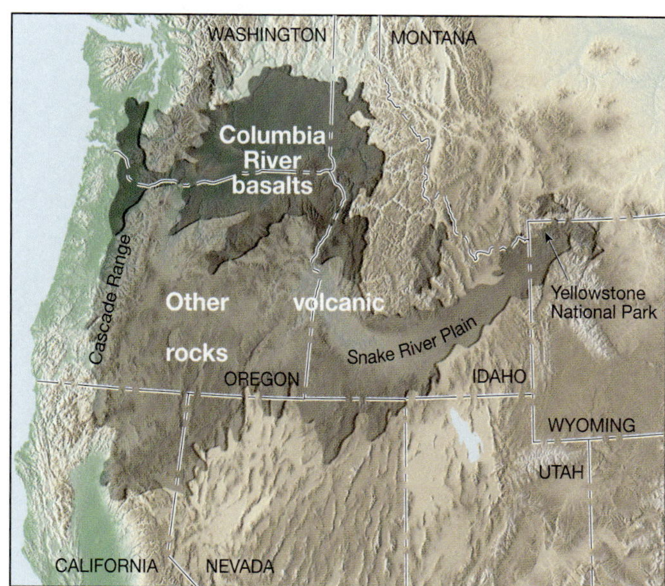

Figure 7.19 Volcanic areas in the northwestern United States.

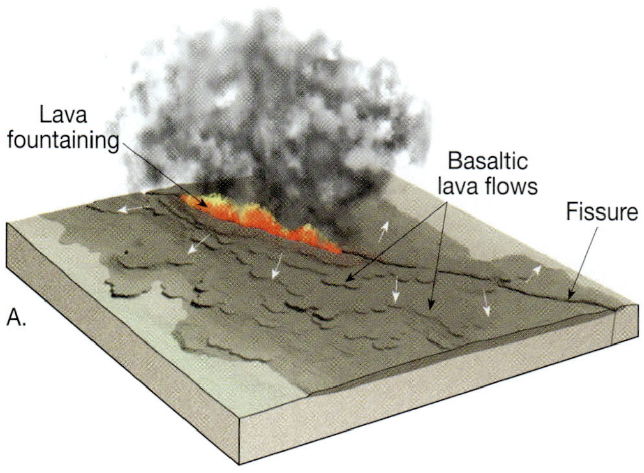

Figure 7.20 A Flood basalts.

NOTES:

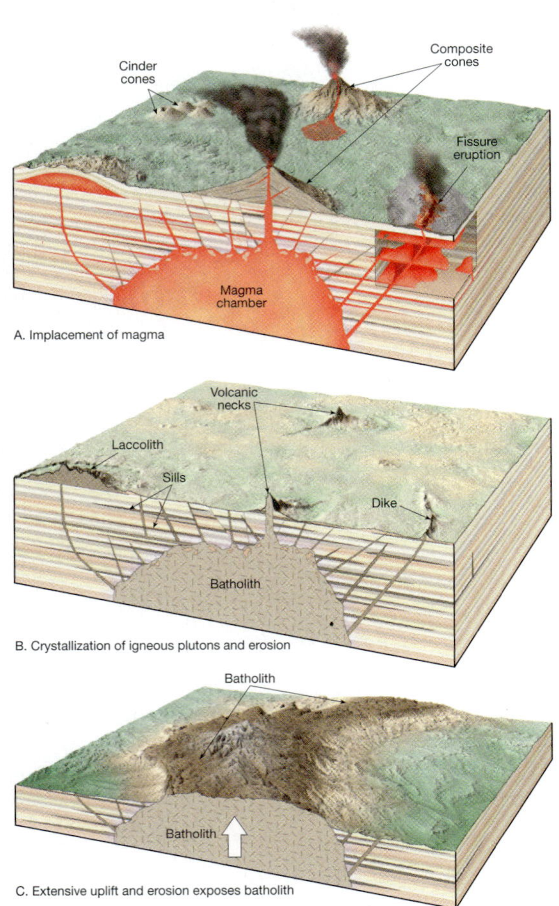

Figure 7.22 **Basic igneous structures.**

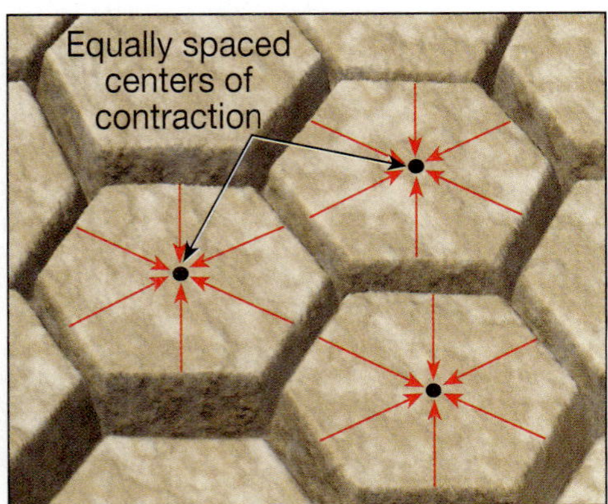

Figure 7.24 **Columnar jointing.**

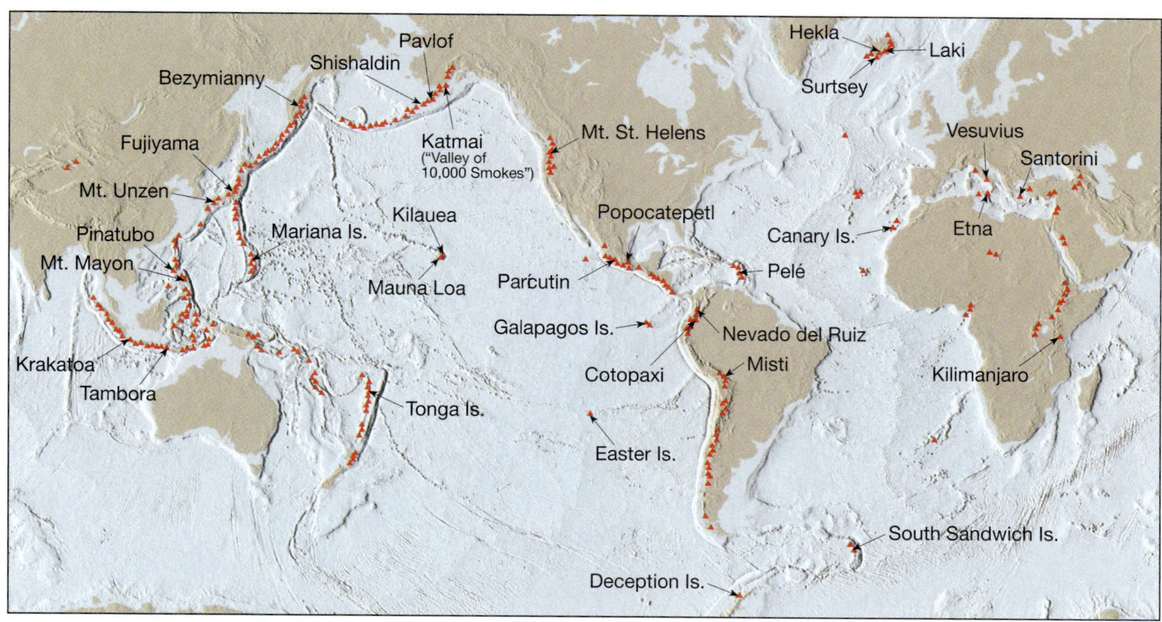

Figure 7.26 **Locations of major volcanoes.**

NOTES:

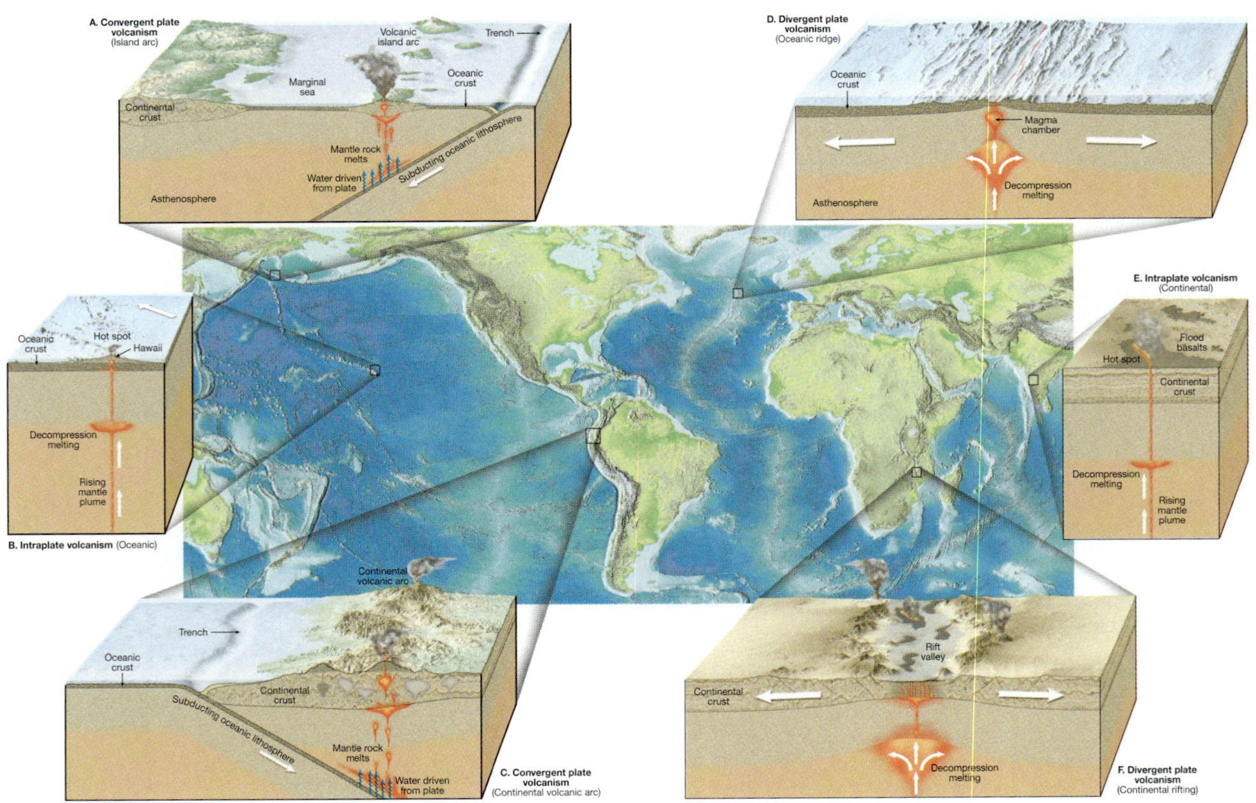

Figure 7.27 **Three zones of volcanism.**

NOTES:

NOTES:

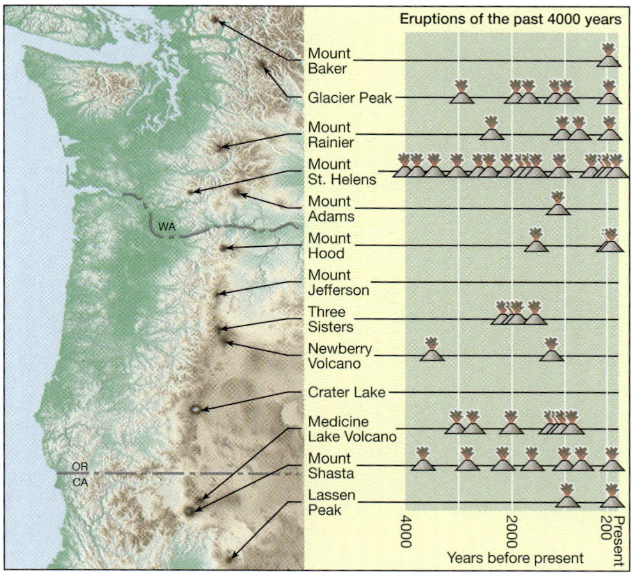

Figure 7.28 **History of Cascade volcanism.**

NOTES:

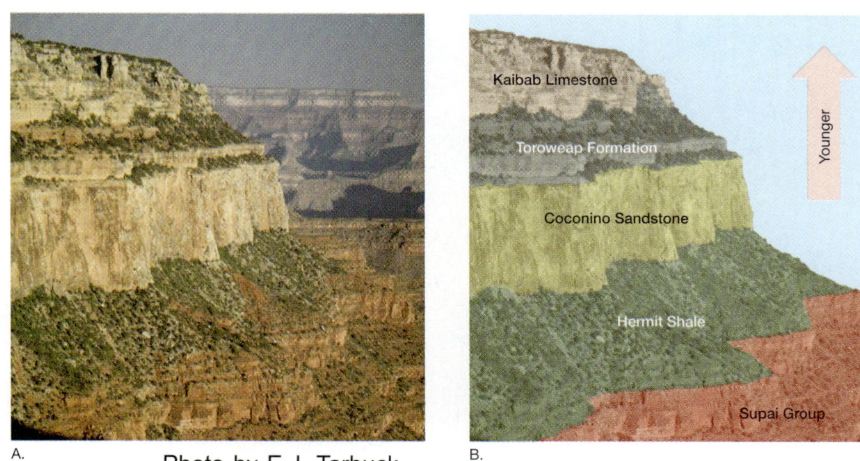

Photo by E.J. Tarbuck

Figure 8.2 Applying the law of superposition.

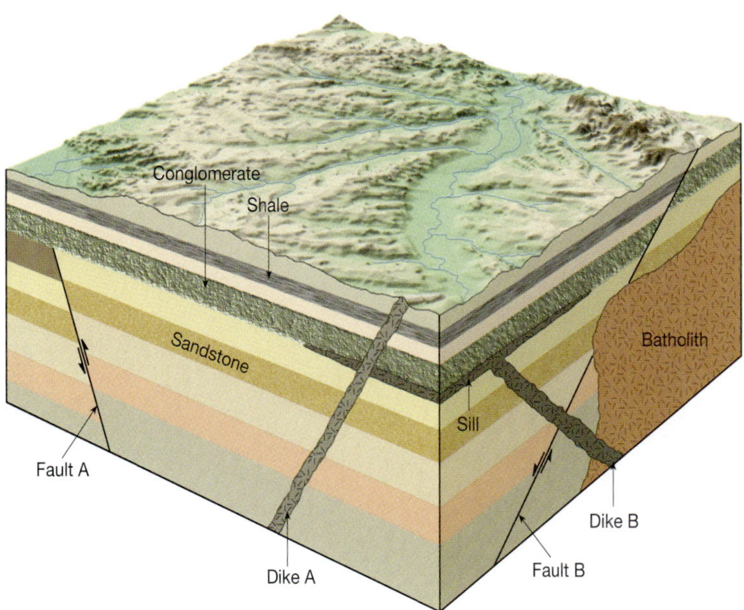

Figure 8.4 Cross-cutting relationships.

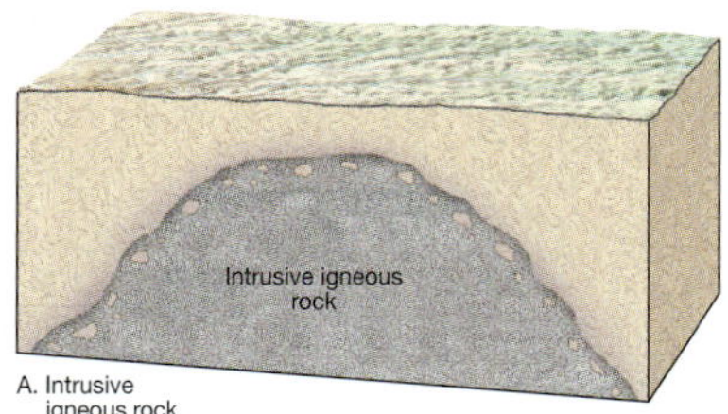

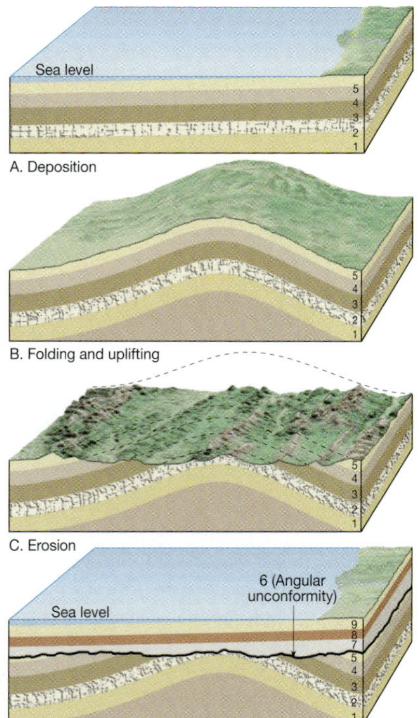

Figure 8.5 Inclusions and nonconformities.

Figure 8.6 A,B,C,D Formation of an angular unconformity.

NOTES:

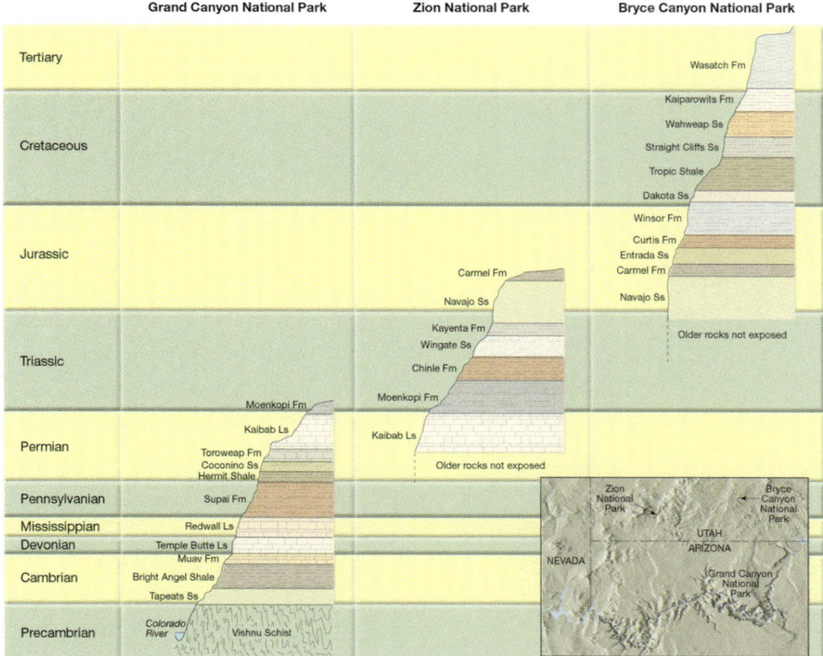

Figure 8.7 Geologic cross section of a hypothetical region.

Figure 8.8 Correlation of strata at three locations on the Colorado Plateau.

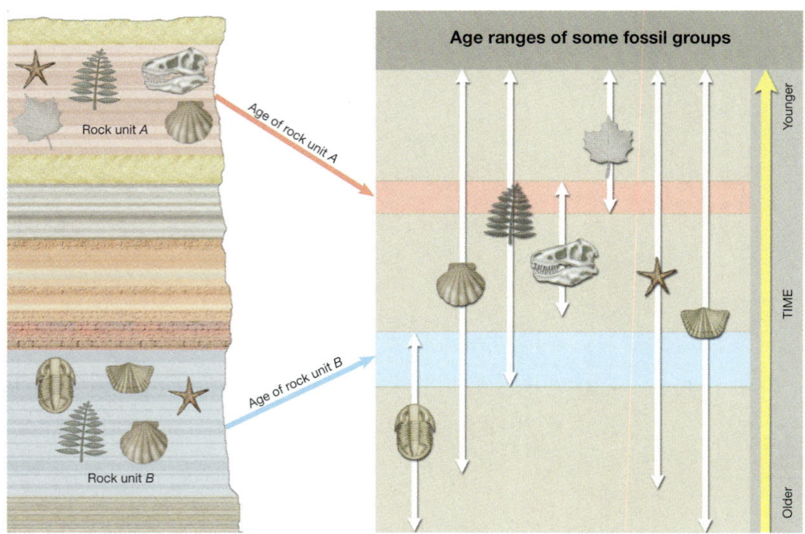

Figure 8.10 Overlapping ranges of fossils.

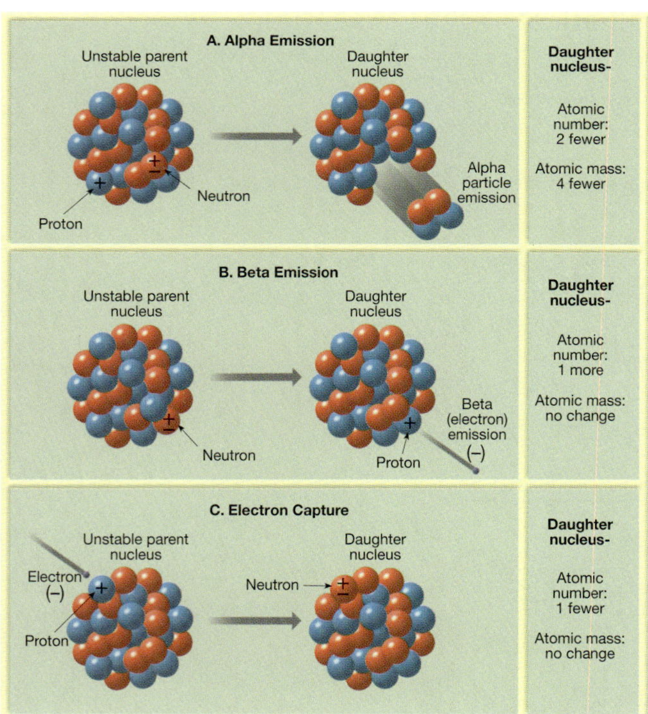

Figure 8.11 Common types of radioactive decay.

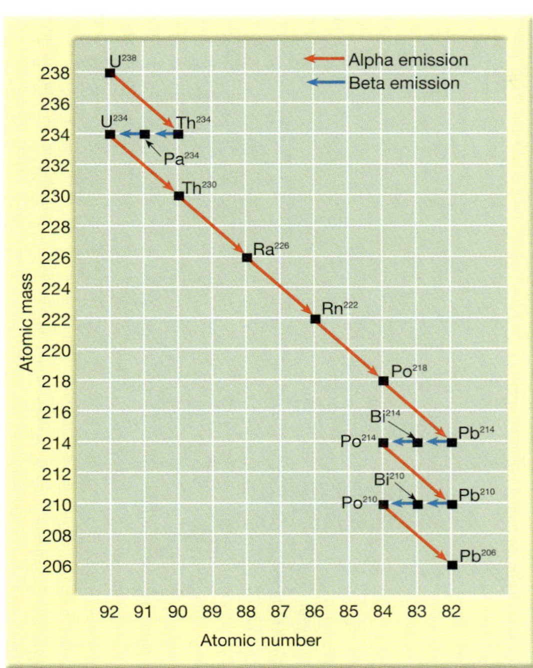

Figure 8.12 Uranium (U-238) is an example of a radioactive decay series.

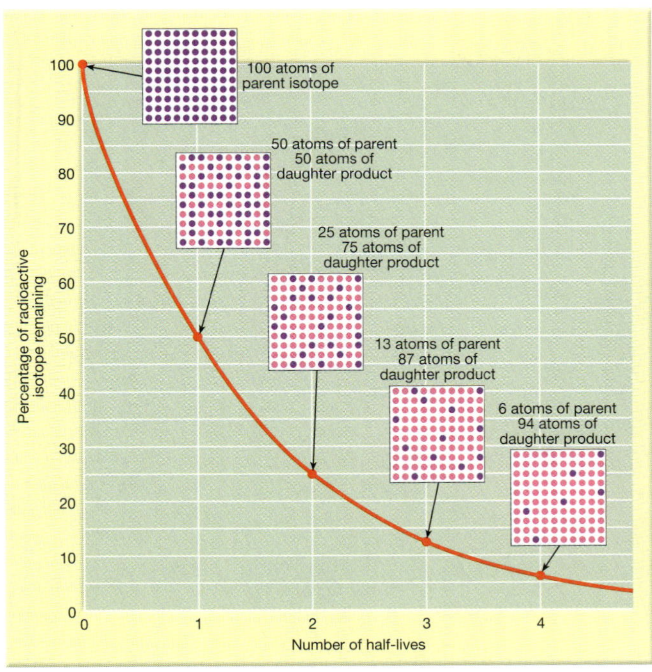

Figure 8.13 Radioactive decay curve.

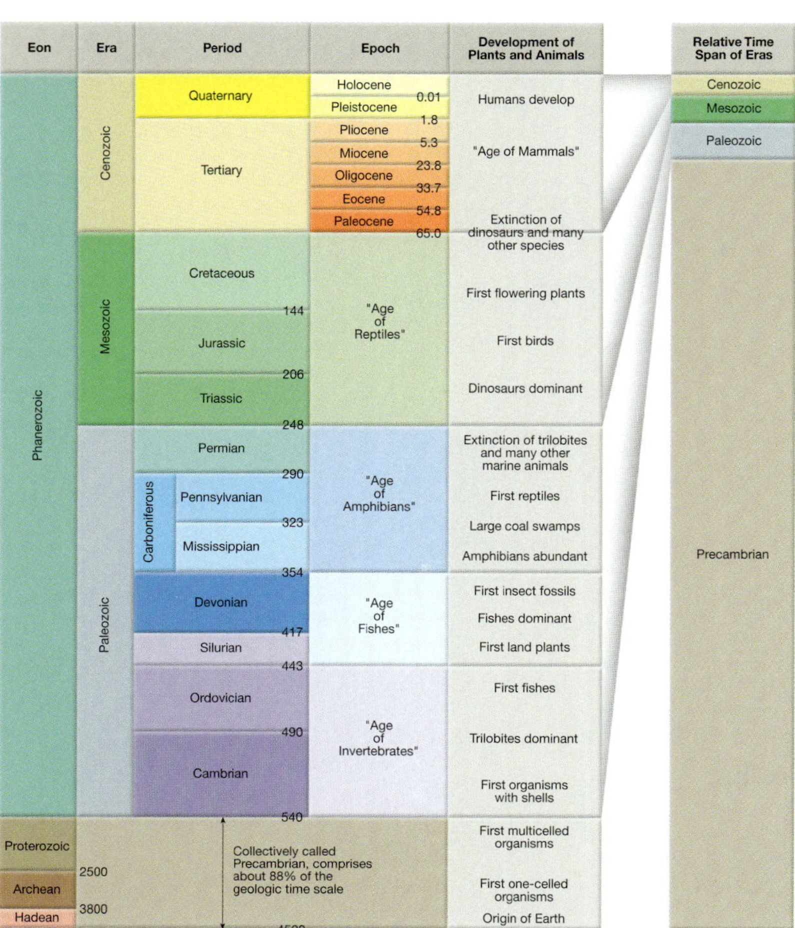

Figure 8.14 The geologic time scale.

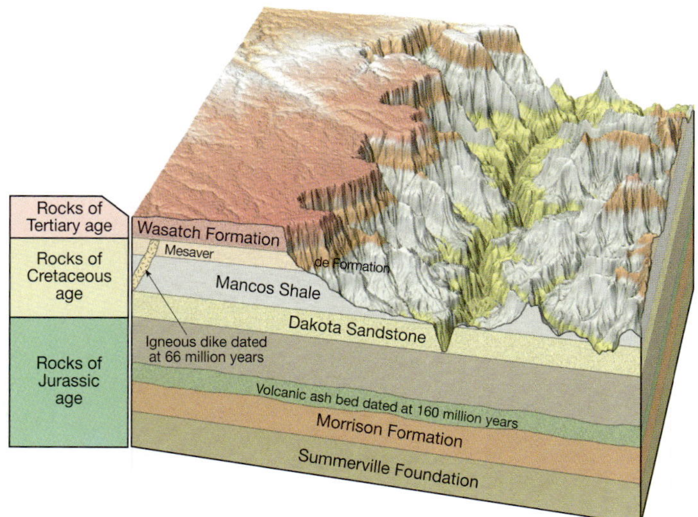

Figure 8.16 Numerical dates for sedimentary layers.

NOTES:

Figure 9.1 Distribution of land and water between the Northern and Southern hemispheres.

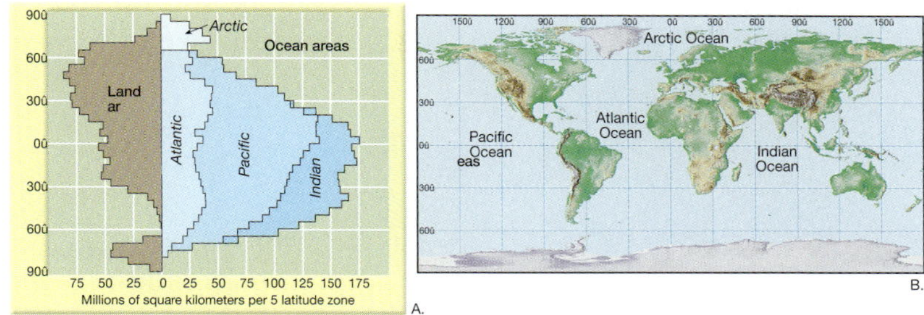

Figure 9.2 Distribution of land and water.

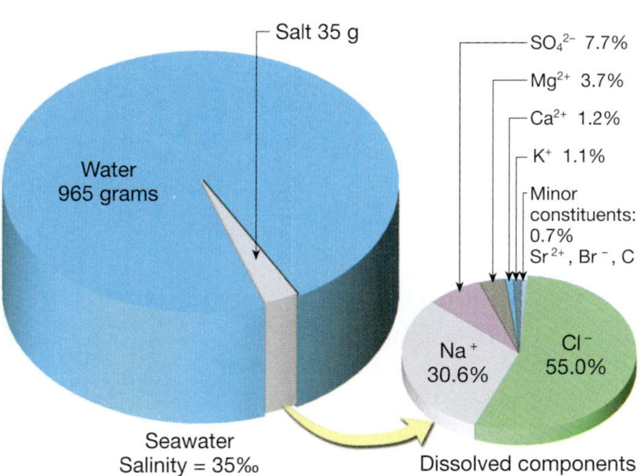

Figure 9.3 Relative proportions of water and dissolved components in seawater.

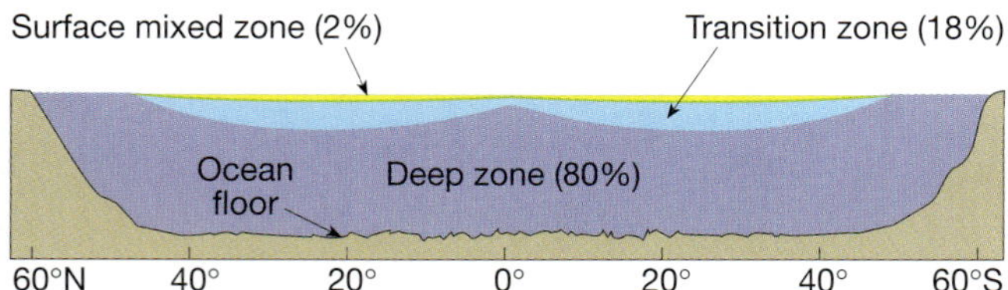

Figure 9.5 Layered structure of the ocean.

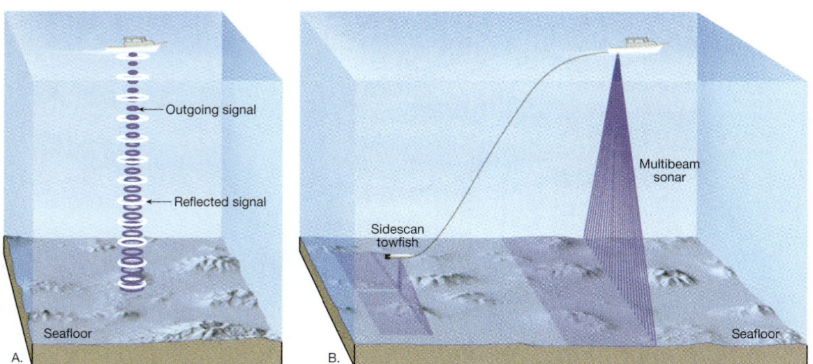

Figure 9.6 Various types of sonar.

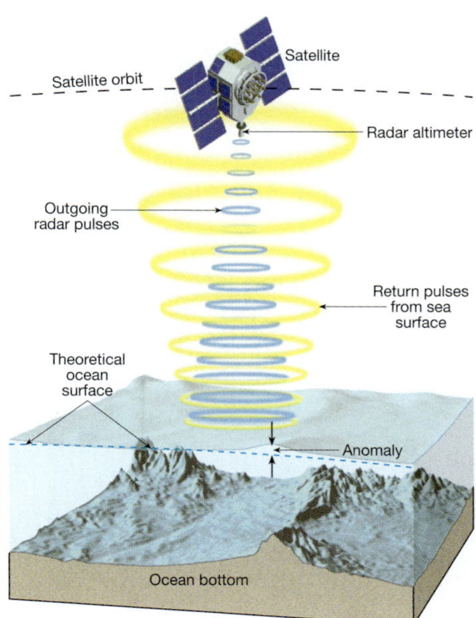

Figure 9.7 A satellite altimeter measures the variation in sea surface elevation.

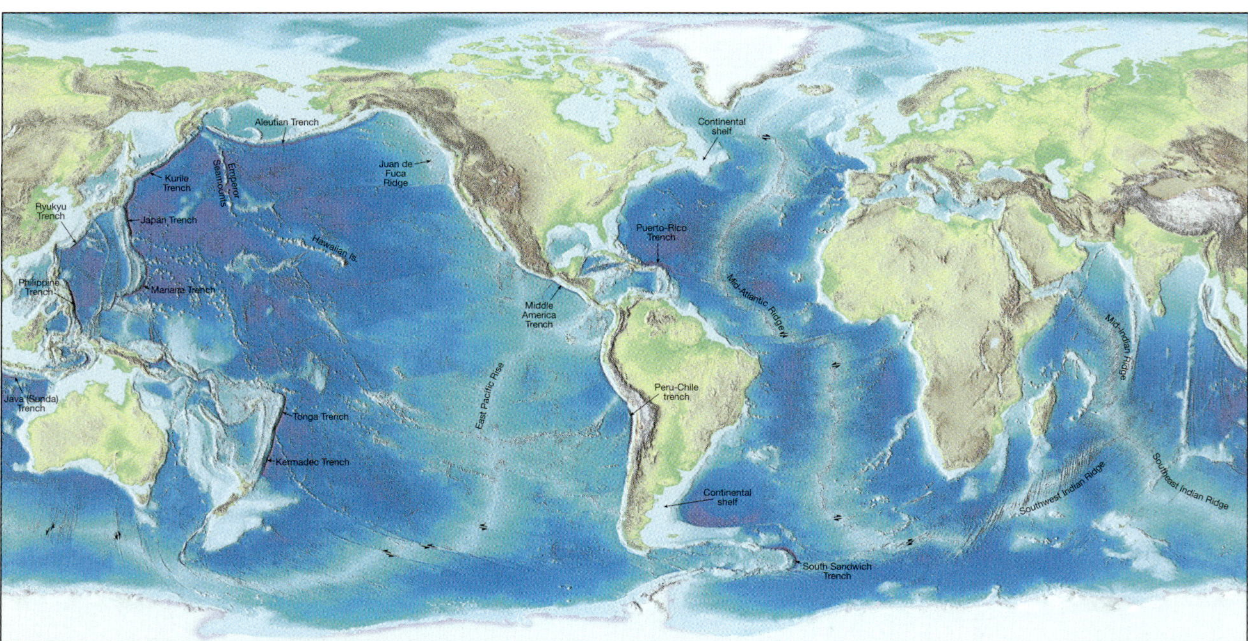

Figure 9.8 The topography of Earth's solid surface.

NOTES:

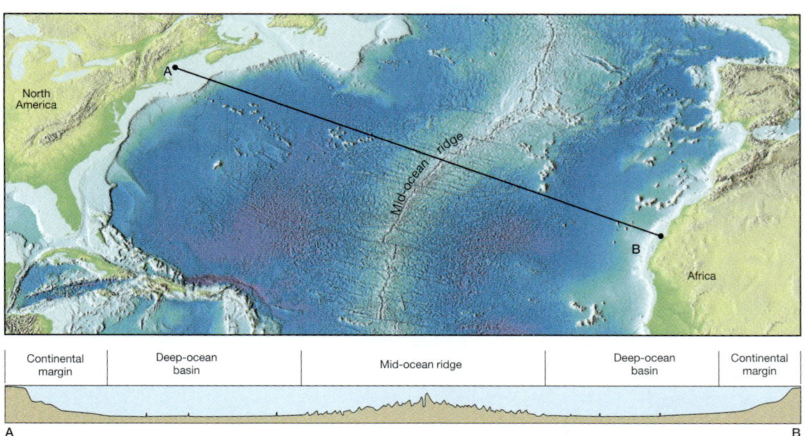

Figure 9.9 Major topographic divisions of the North Atlantic Ocean.

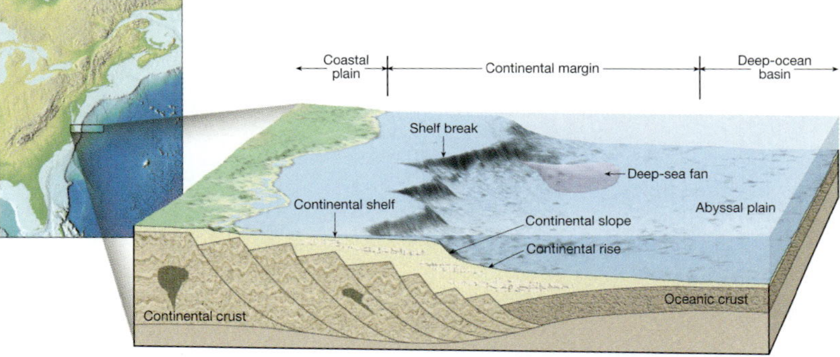

Figure 9.10 Parts of the passive continental margin.

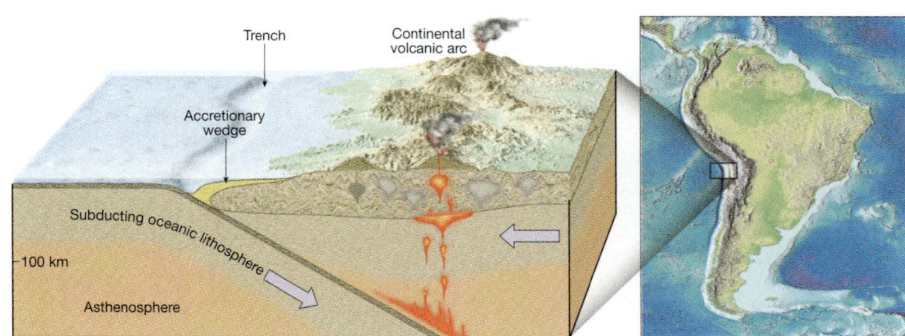

Figure 9.11 Active continental margin.

NOTES:

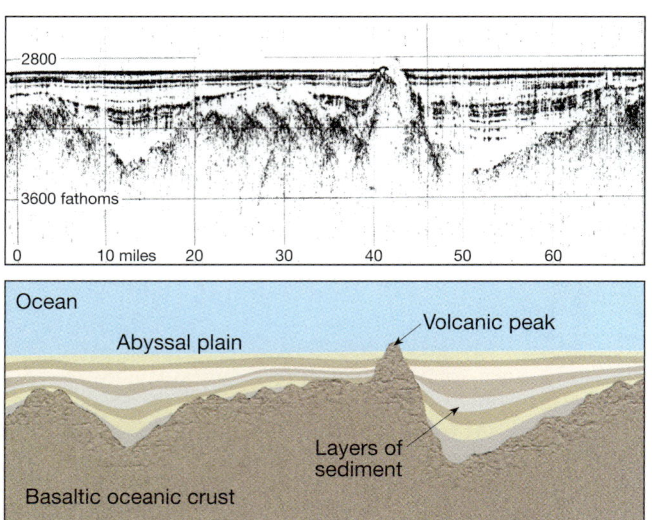

Figure 9.12 Madeira abyssal plain.

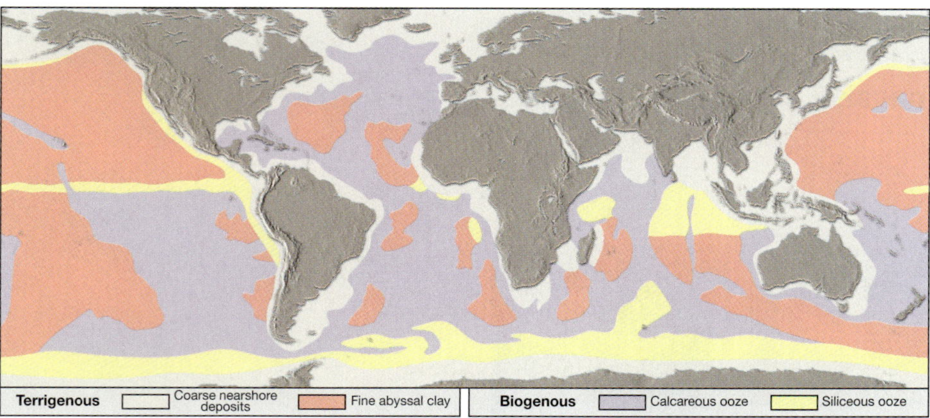

Figure 9.15 Distribution of marine sediment.

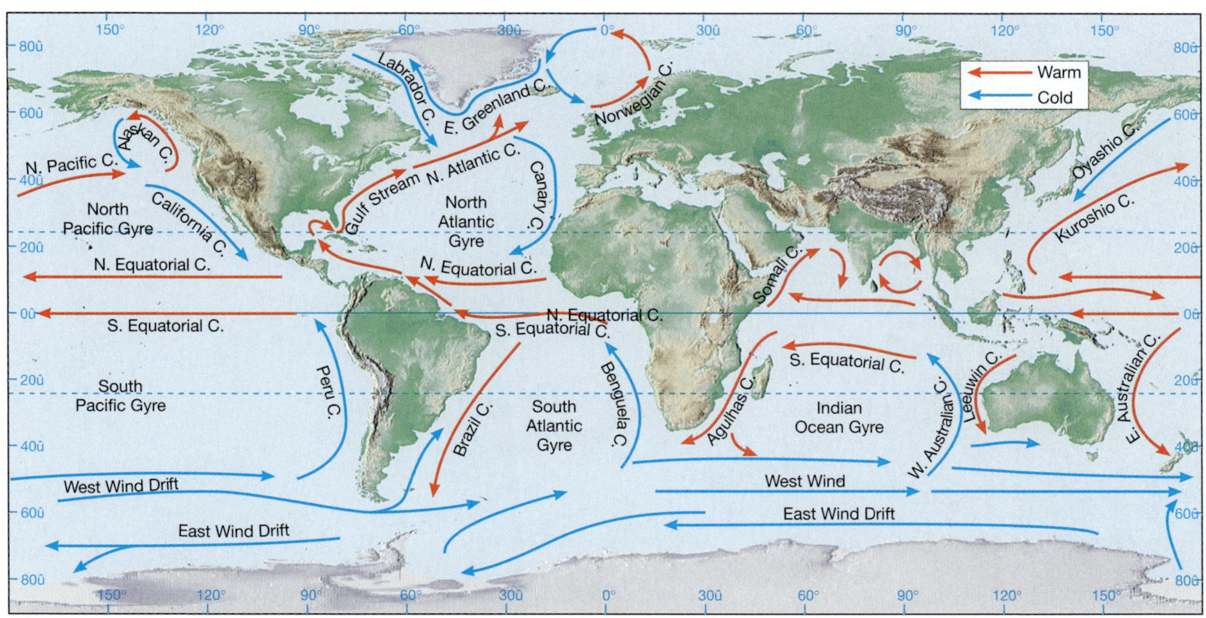

Figure 10.2 Average ocean surface currents.

NOTES:

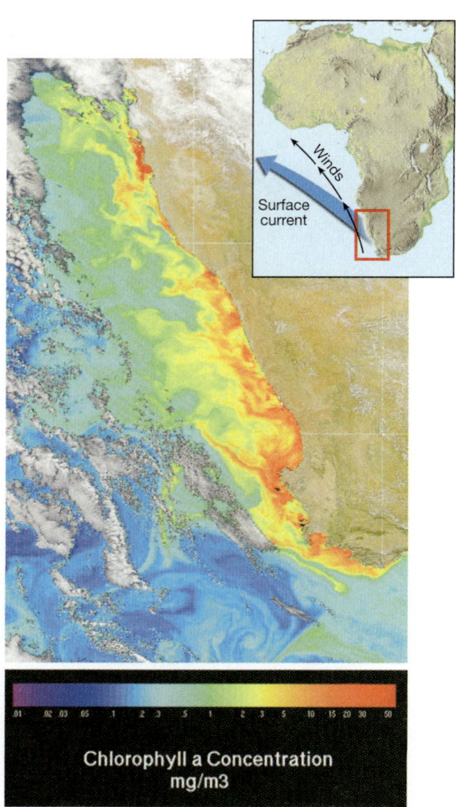

Figure 10.4 Coastal upwelling.

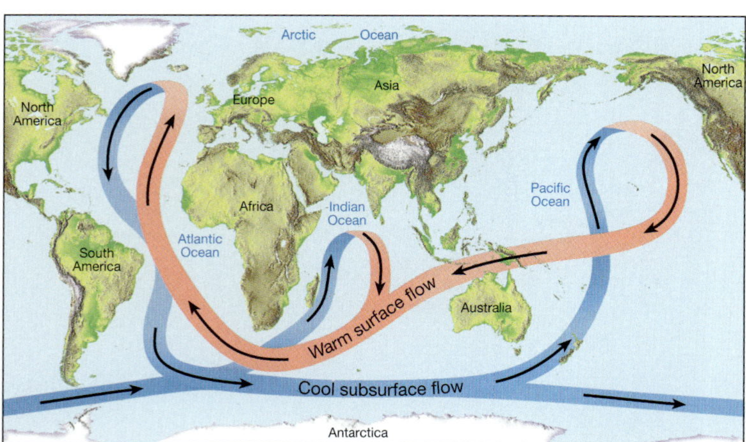

Figure 10.6 Idealized "conveyor belt" model of ocean circulation.

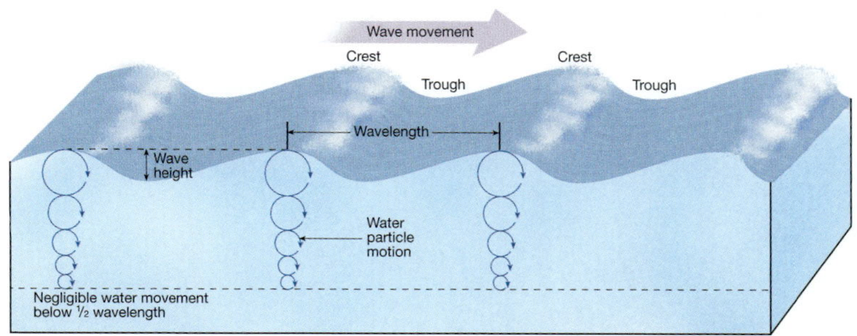

Figure 10.7 Diagrammatic view of an idealized non-breaking ocean wave.

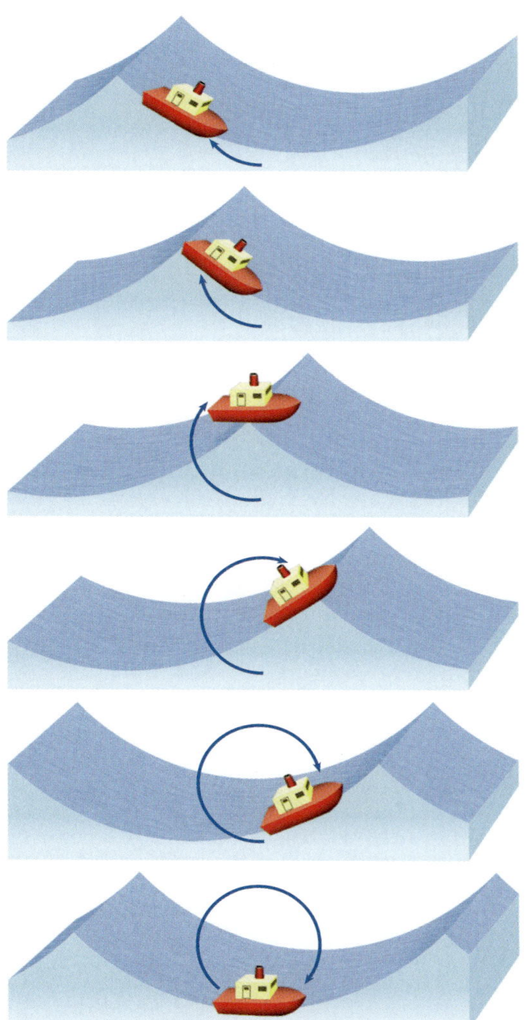

Figure 10.8 Circular orbital motion of waves.

NOTES:

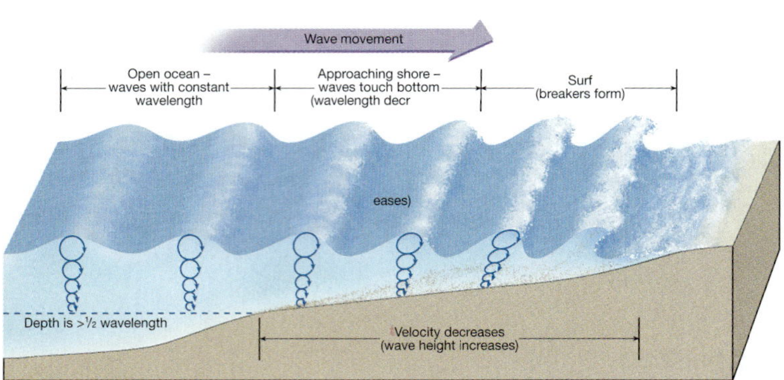

Figure 10.9 Changes that occur when a wave moves onto shore.

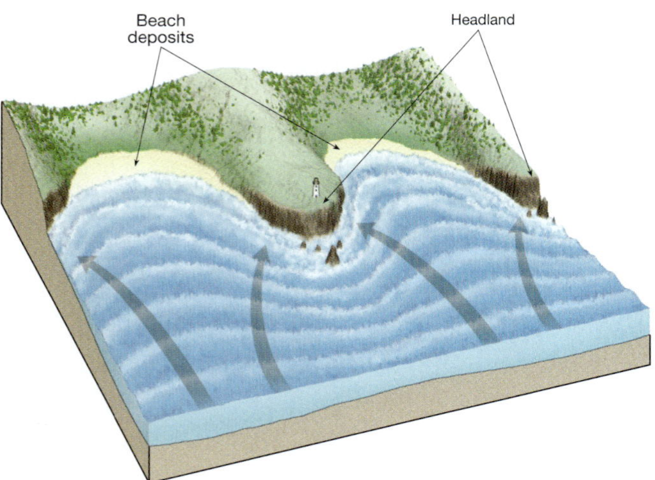

Figure 10.12 Wave refraction.

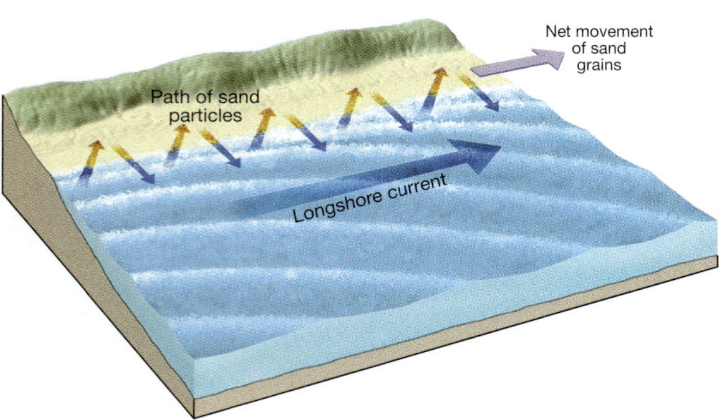

Figure 10.13 Beach drift and longshore currents.

Figure 10.17 Barrier islands rim the Gulf and Atlantic Coasts.

Figure 10.18 Evolution of an initially irregular coastline.

Figure 10.23 Major estuaries along the East Coast of the United States.

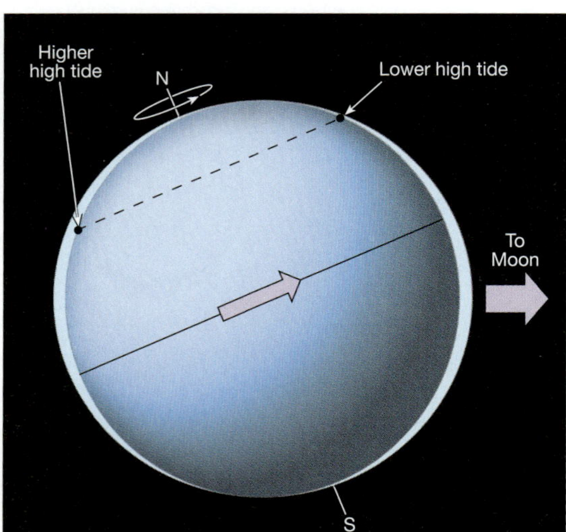

Figure 10.25 Idealized tidal bulges.

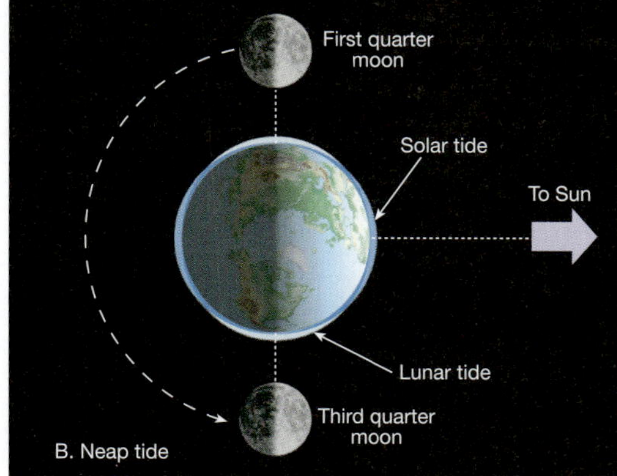

Figure 10.26 Earth-Moon-Sun positions and the tides.

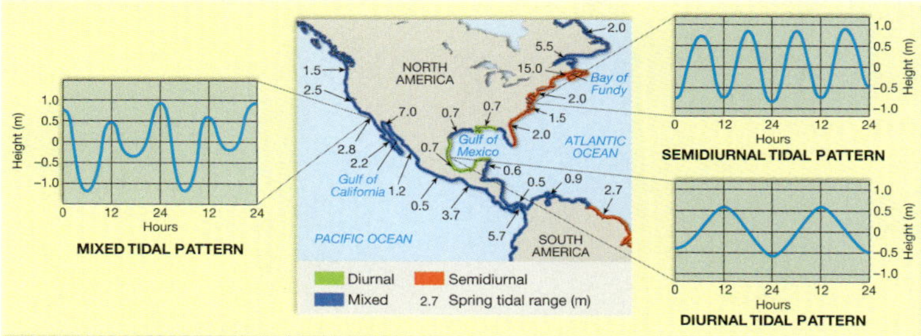

Figure 10.27 Tidal patterns.

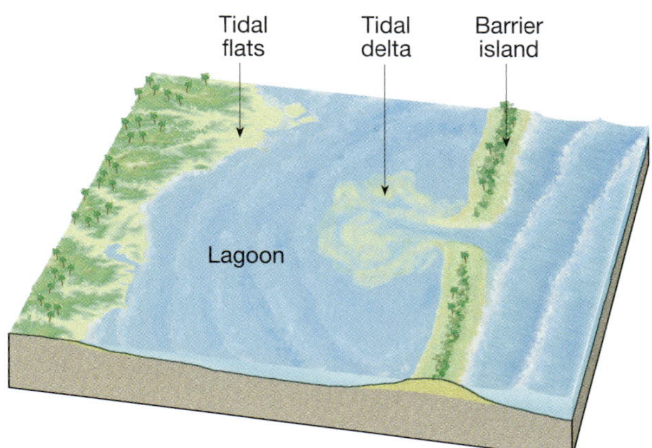

Figure 10.28 Tidal delta.

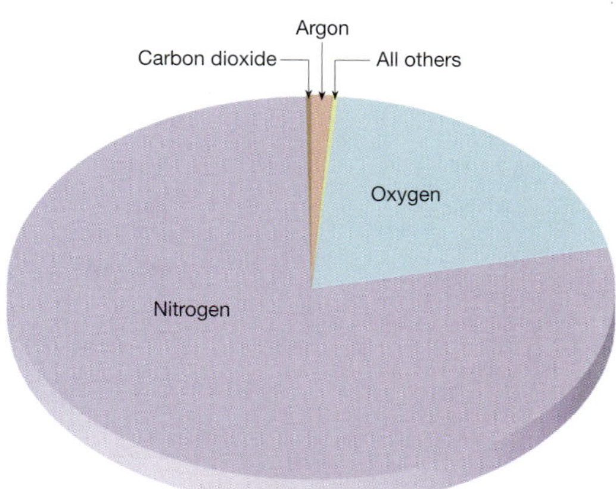

Figure 11.2 Proportional volume of gases composing dry air.

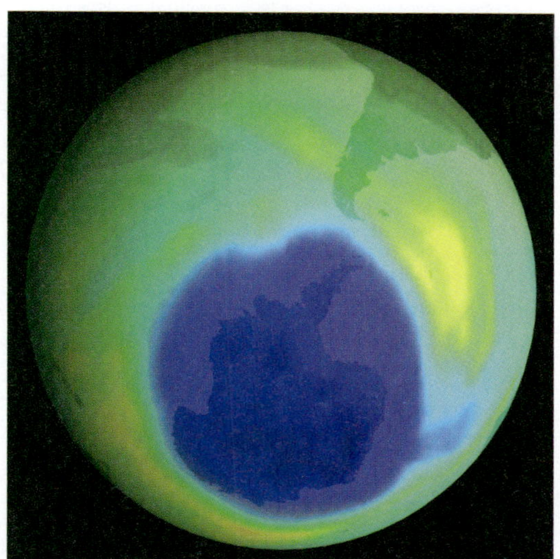

Figure 11.4 Ozone distribution in the Southern hemisphere.

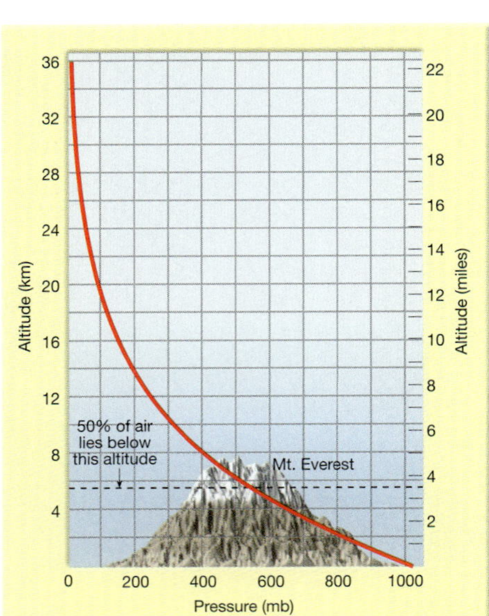

Figure 11.5 Atmospheric pressure variation with altitude.

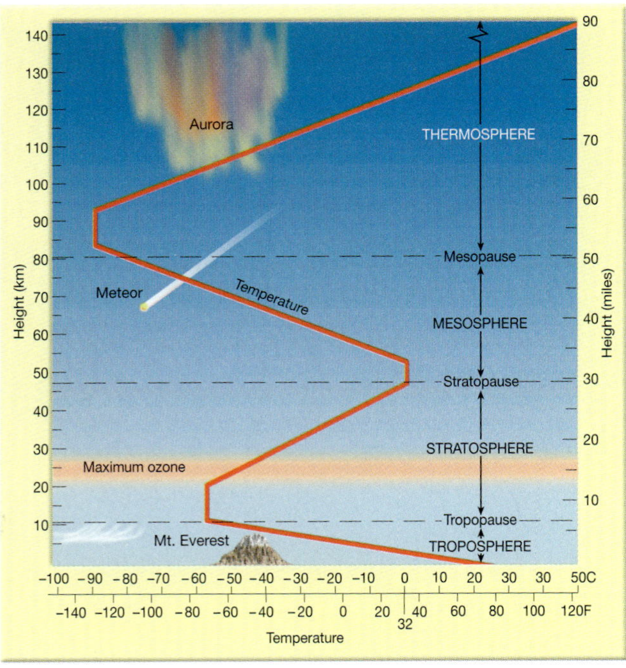

Figure 11.7 Thermal structure of the atmosphere.

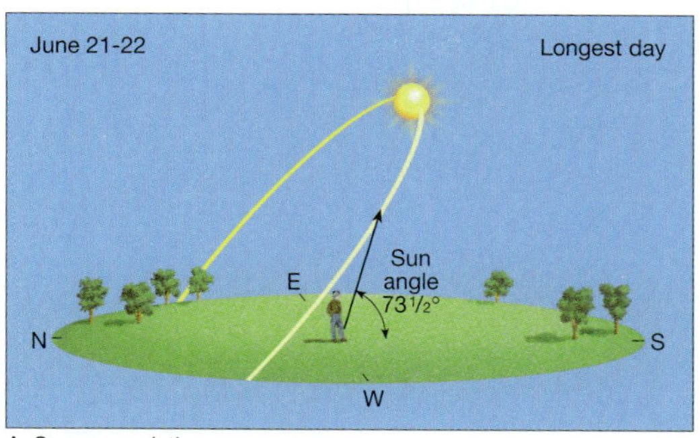

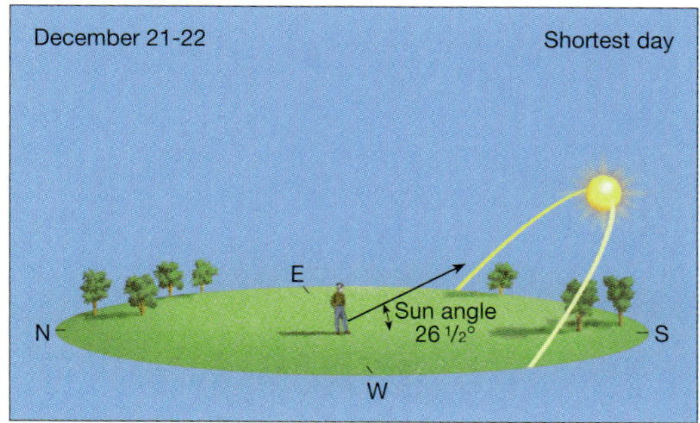

Figure 11.9 Daily paths of the Sun for a place located at 40° N latitude.

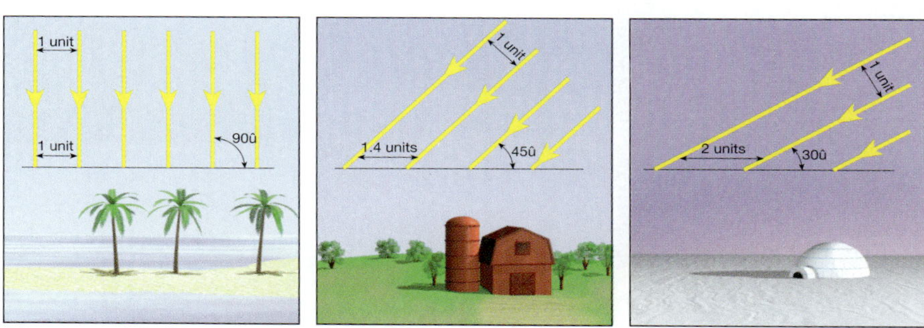

Figure 11.10 Changes in the Sun's angle.

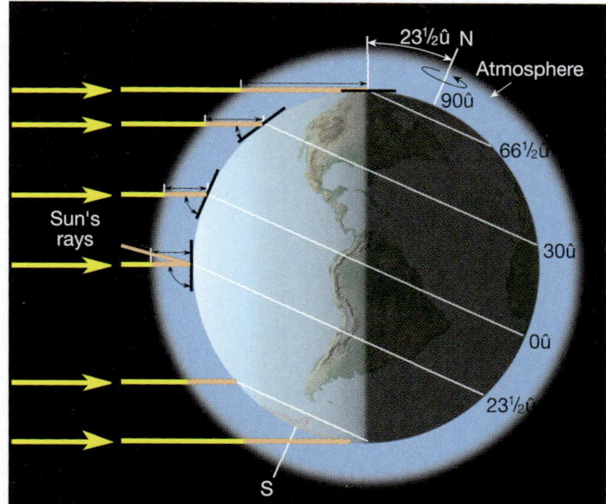

Figure 11.11 Influence of Sun angle on albedo.

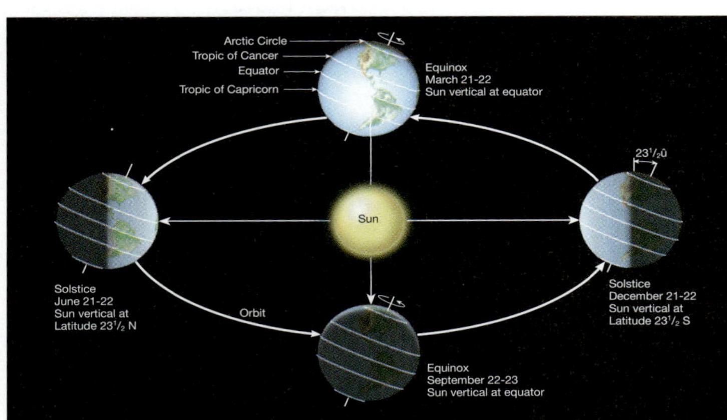

Figure 11.12 Earth-Sun relationships.

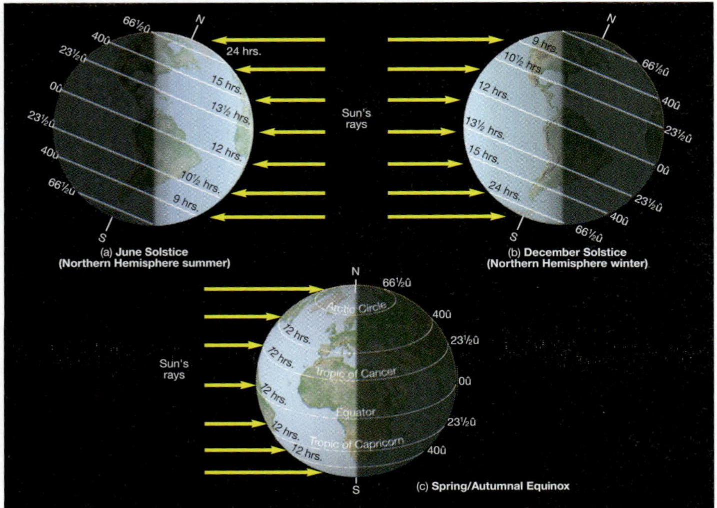

Figure 11.13 Characteristics of the solstices and equinoxes.

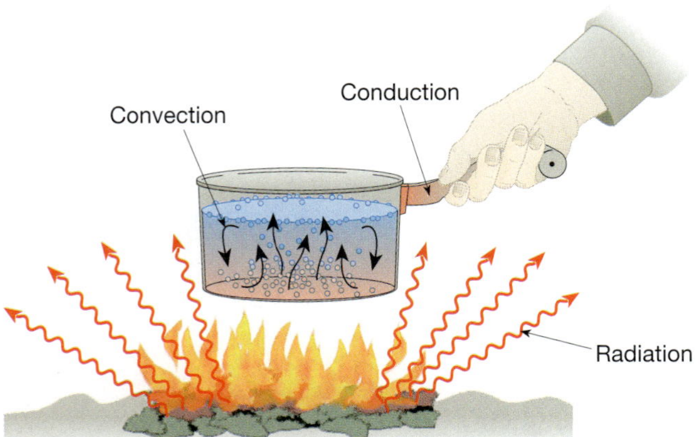

Figure 11.14 Three mechanisms of heat transfer.

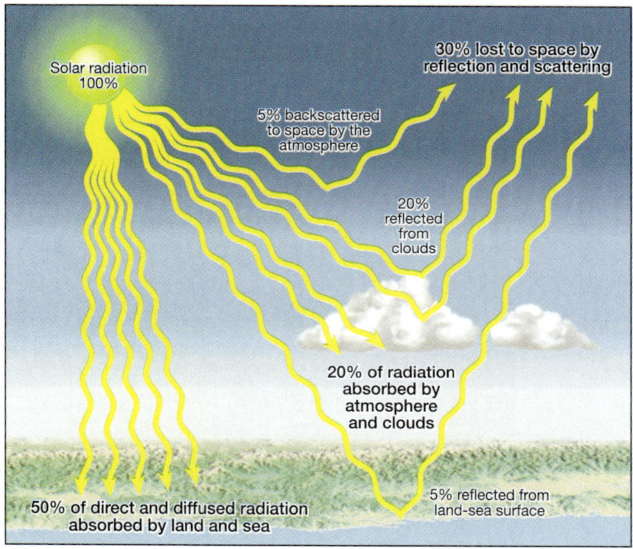

Figure 11.15 **The electromagnetic spectrum.**

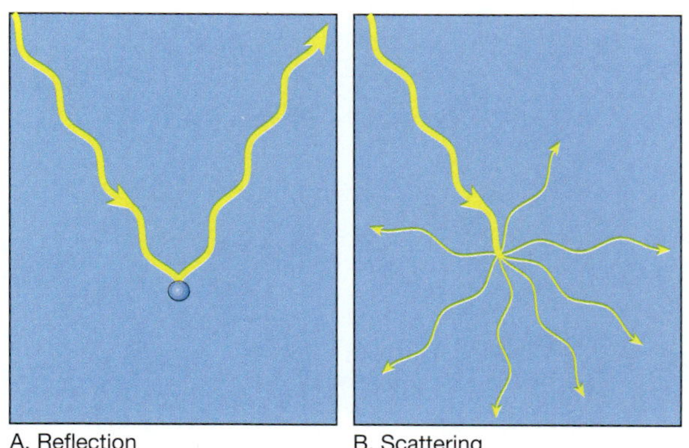

Figure 11.17 **Average distribution of incoming solar radiation by percentage.**

Figure 11.18 **Reflection and scattering.**

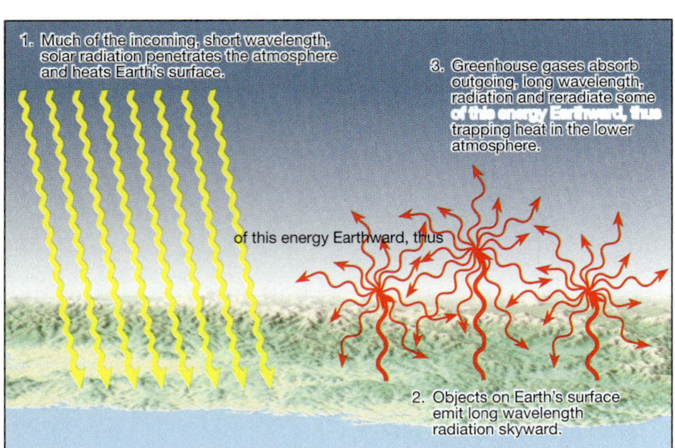

Figure 11.19 The heating of the atmosphere.

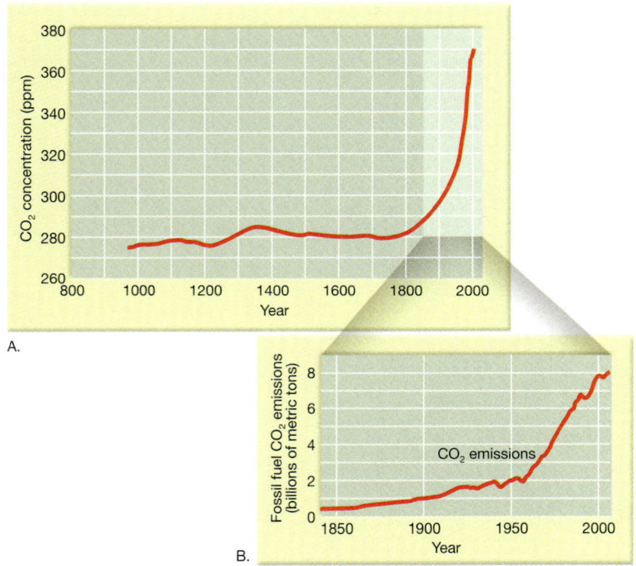

Figure 11.20 Carbon dioxide concentrations and emissions.

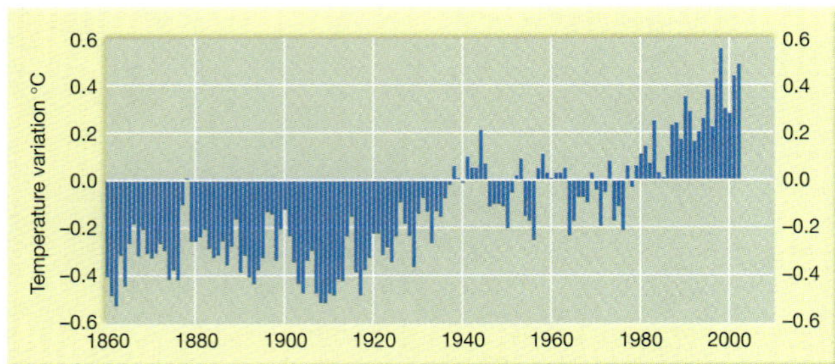

Figure 11.21 Annual average global temp- erature variations for the period 1860-2002.

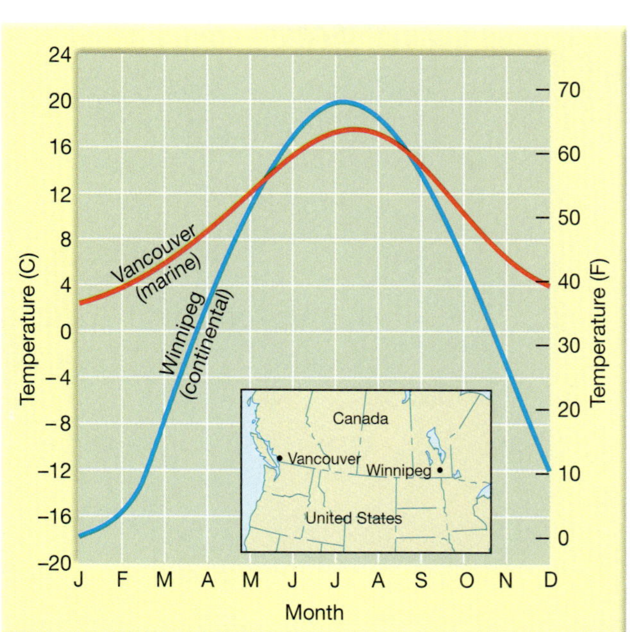

Figure 11.23 Mean monthly temperatures for Vancouver, British Columbia, and Winnipeg, Manitoba.

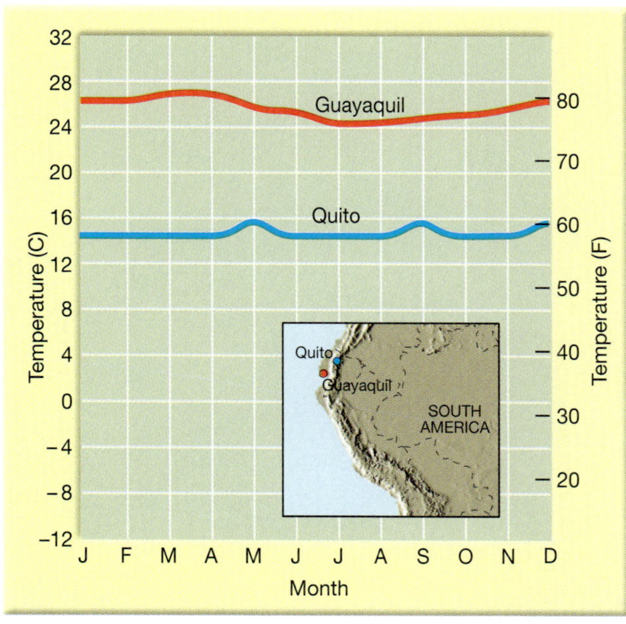

Figure 11.24 Temperatures at Quito vs. Guayaquil.

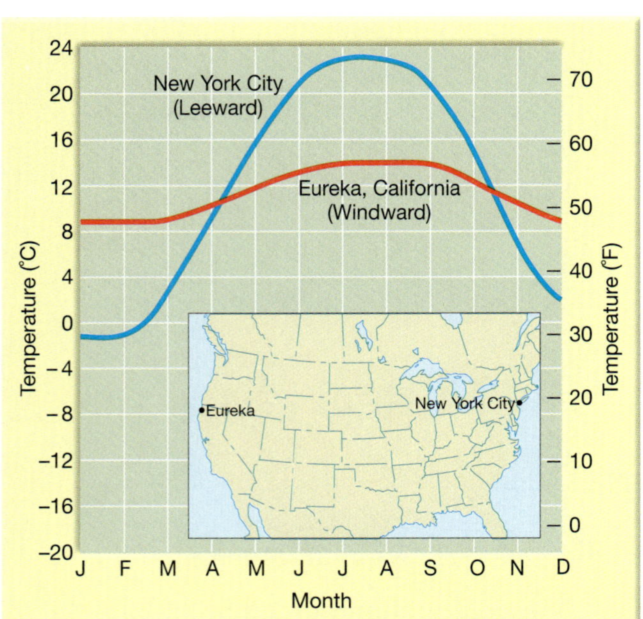

Figure 11.25 Temperatures at Eureka, CA vs. New York City.

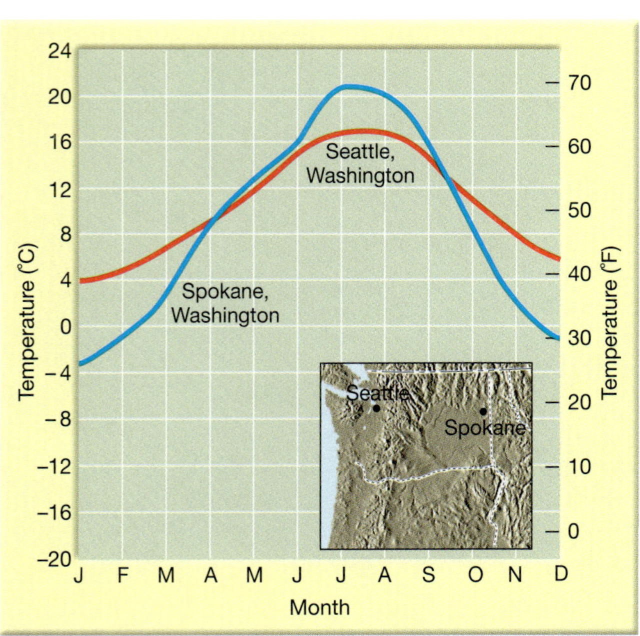

Figure 11.26 Temperatures at Seattle vs. Spokane.

NOTES:

Figure 11.27 Influence of clouds on daily temperature range.

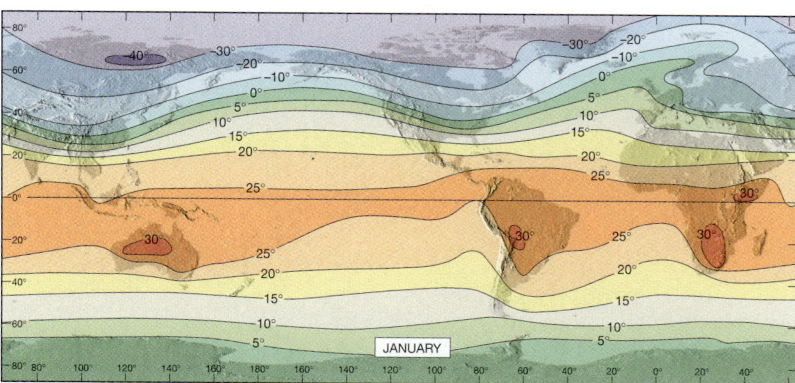

Figure 11.28 World mean sea-level temperatures in January in degrees Celsius.

NOTES:

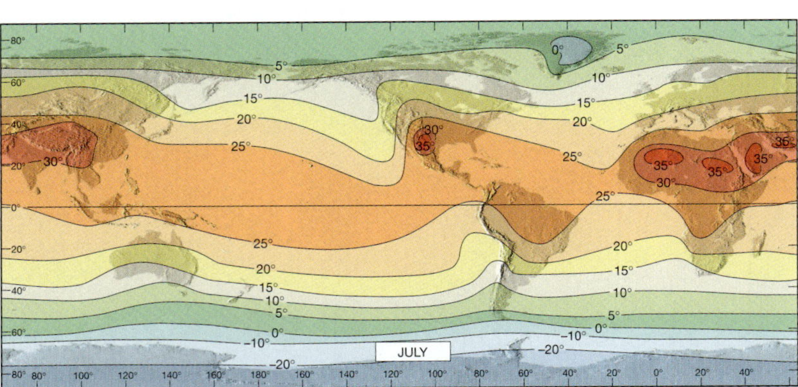

Figure 11.29 World mean sea-level temperatures in July in degrees Celsius.

NOTES:

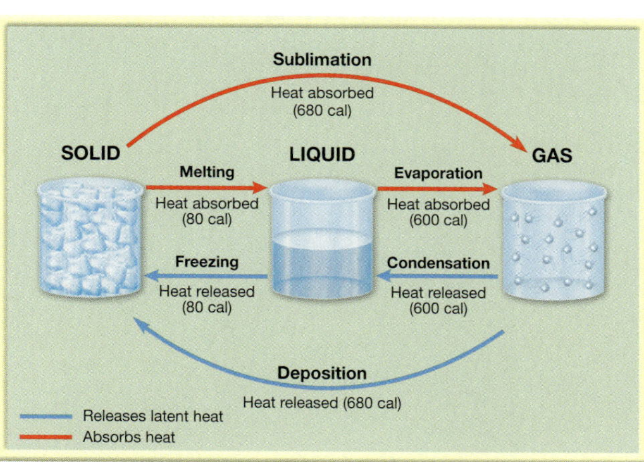

Figure 12.1 Changes of state.

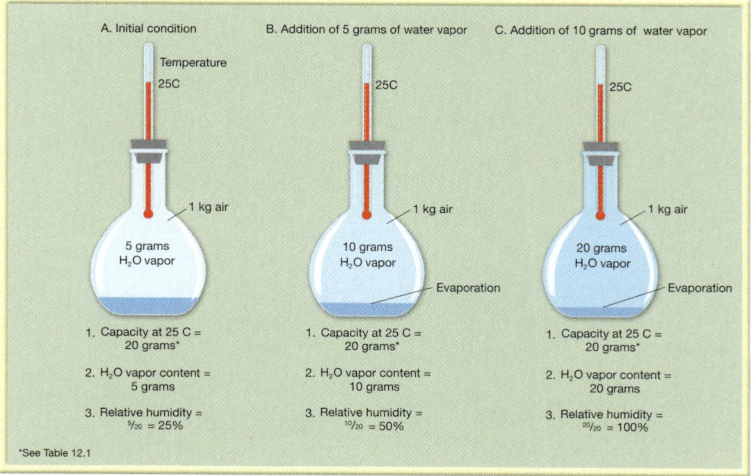

Figure 12.3 Relative humidity varies with variations in mixing ratio.

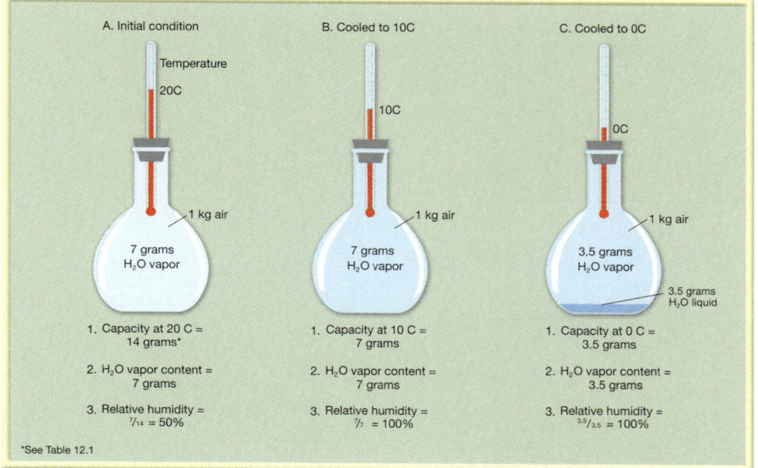

Figure 12.4 Relative humidity varies with temperature.

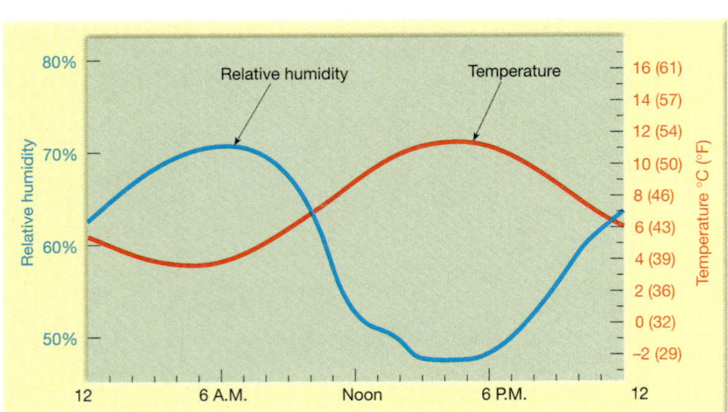

Figure 12.5 Typical daily variations in temperature and relative humidity.

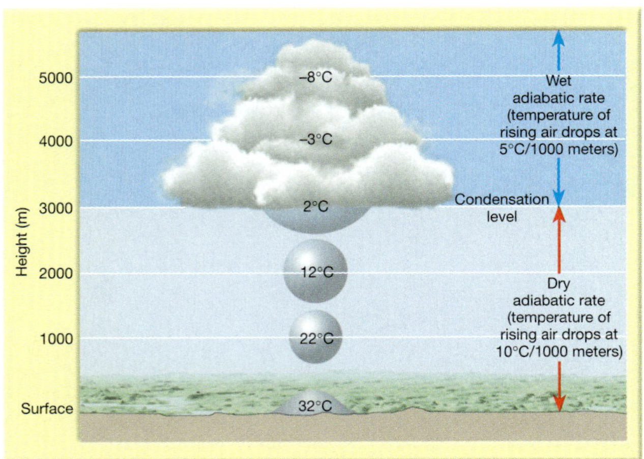

Figure 12.7 Adiabatic cooling and cloud formation.

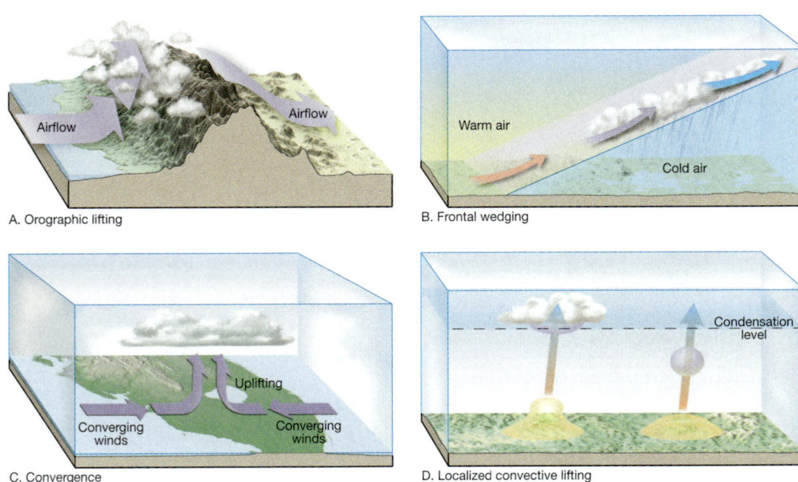

Figure 12.8 Four processes that lift air.

NOTES:

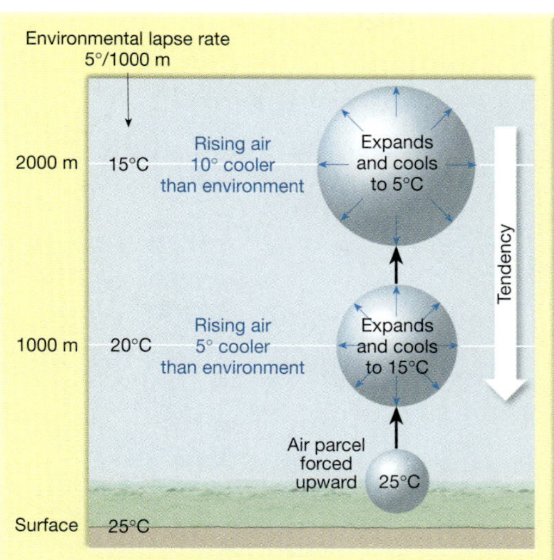

Figure 12.11 Illustration of a stable atmosphere.

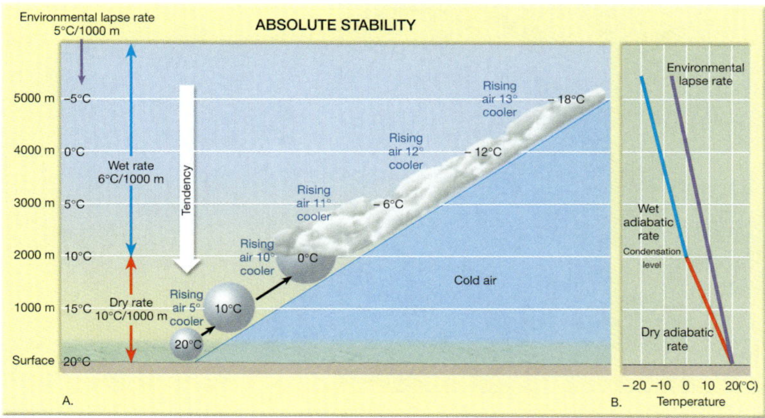

Figure 12.12 Illustration of *absolute stability*.

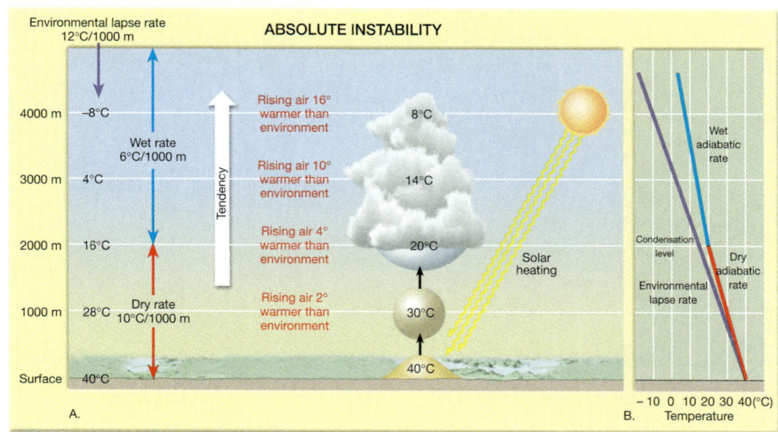

Figure 12.13 Illustration of *absolute instability*.

NOTES:

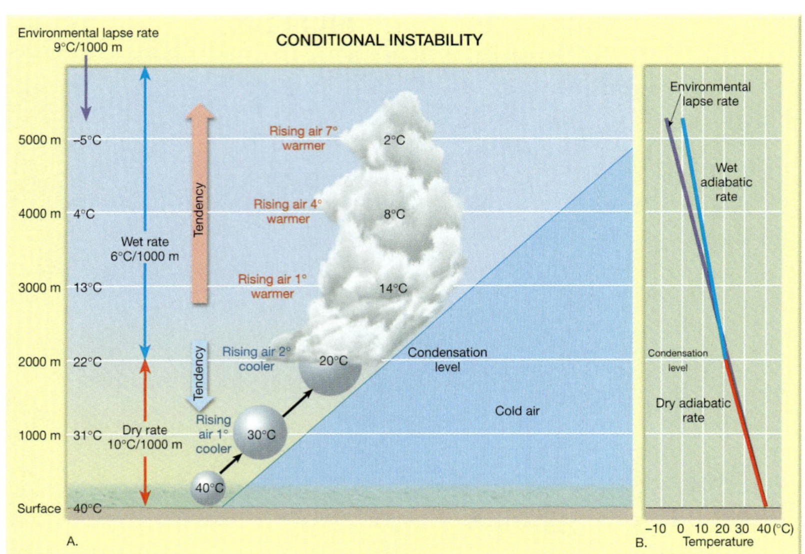

Figure 12.14 Illustration of *conditional instability.*

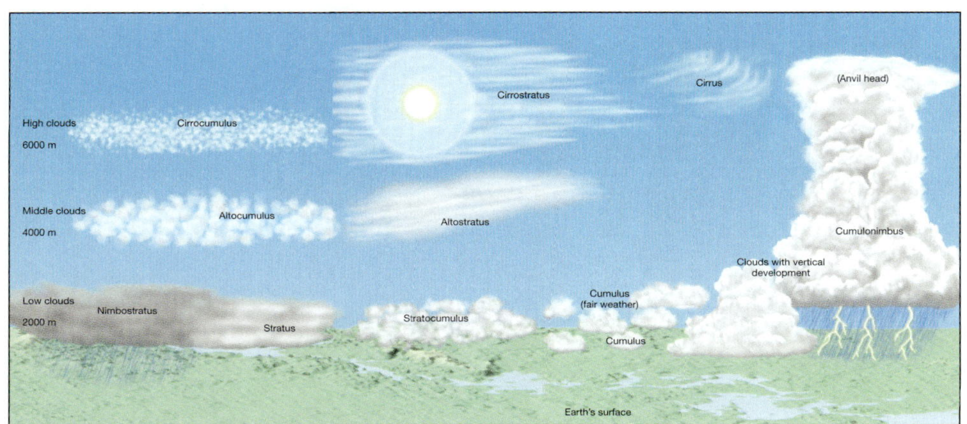

Figure 12.15 Classification of clouds.

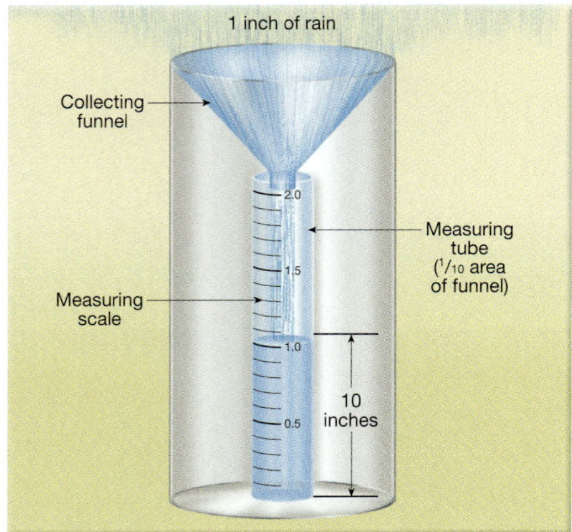

Figure 12.23 Precipitation measurement.

NOTES:

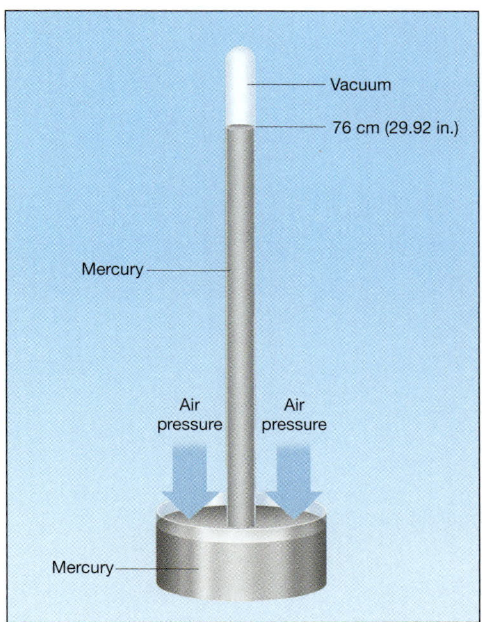

Figure 13.2 Simple mercury barometer.

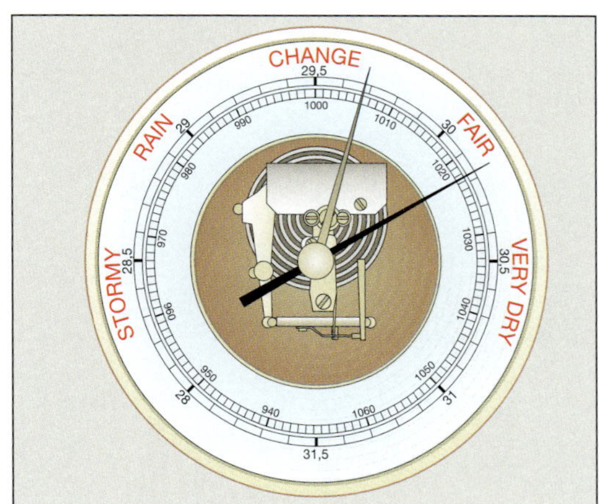

Figure 13.3 Aneroid barometer.

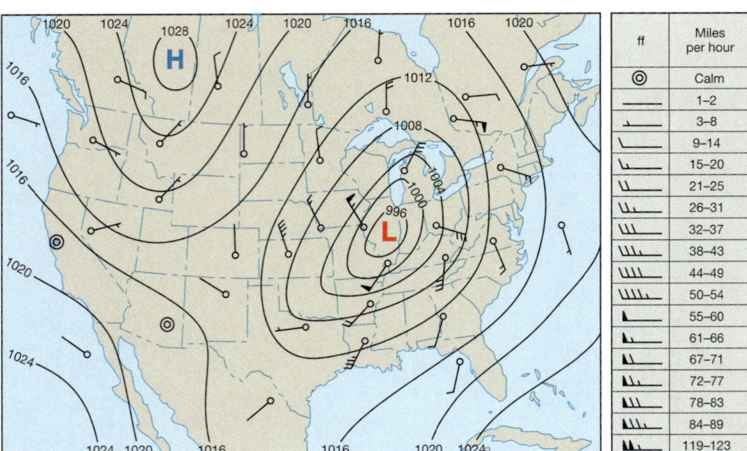

Figure 13.5 Isobars show the distribution of pressure on weather maps.

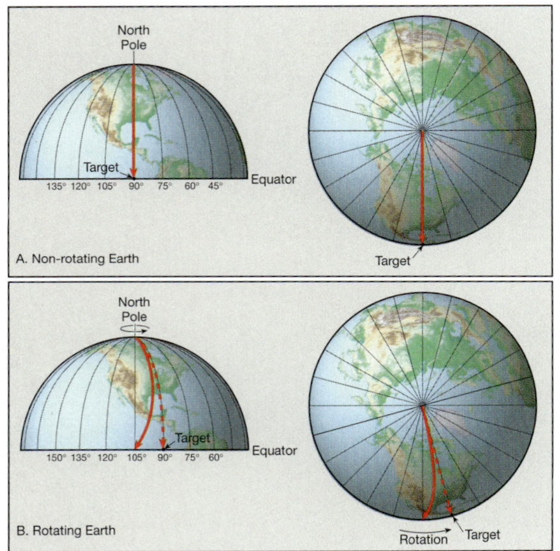

Figure 13.6 The Coriolis effect.

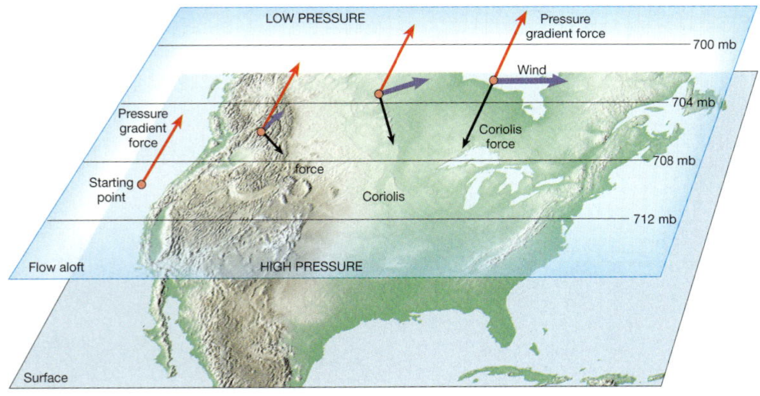

Figure 13.7 The geostrophic wind.

NOTES:

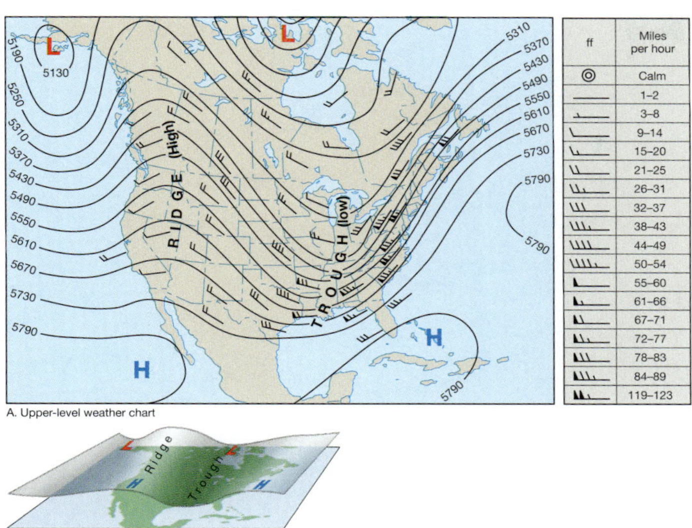

Figure 13.8 Upper-air winds.

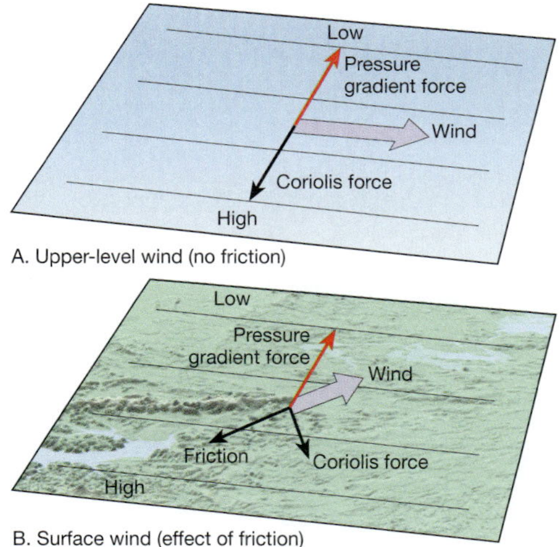

Figure 13.9 Comparison between upper-level winds and surface winds.

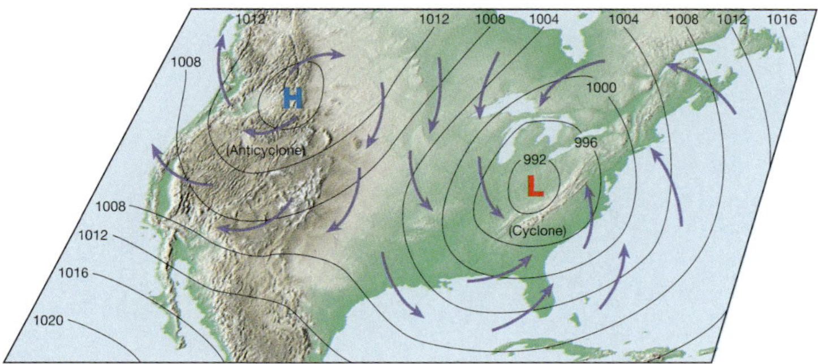

Figure 13.10 Cyclonic and anticyclonic winds in the Northern Hemisphere.

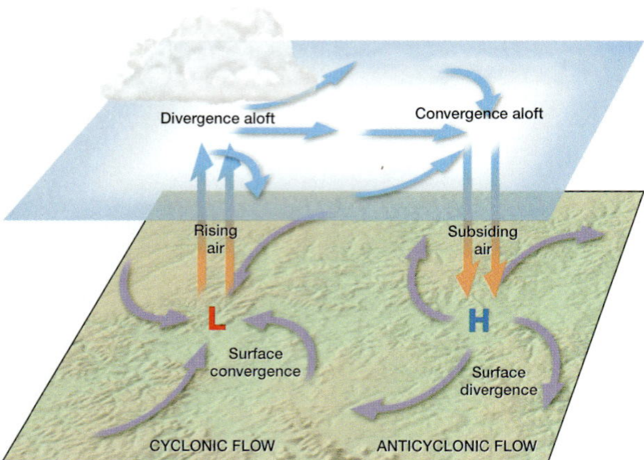

Figure 13.11 Airflow associated with surface cyclones and anticyclones.

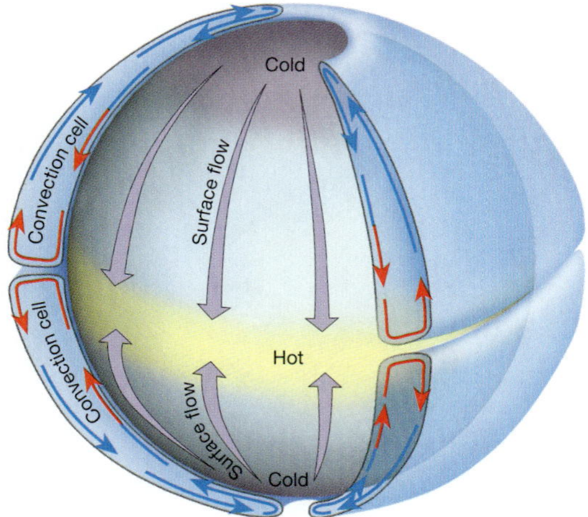

Figure 13.13 Global circulation on a nonrotating Earth.

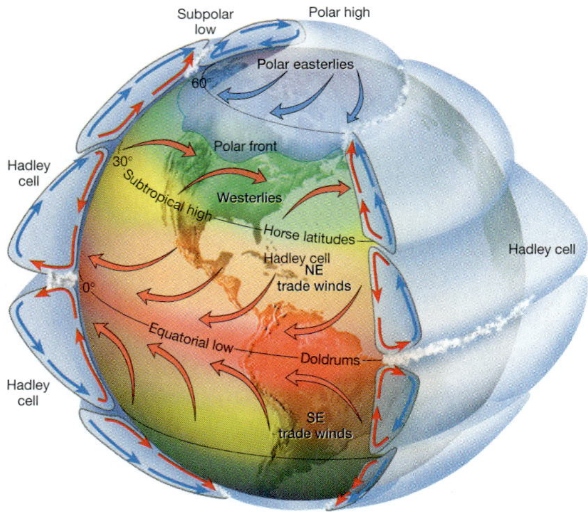

Figure 13.14 Idealized global circulation.

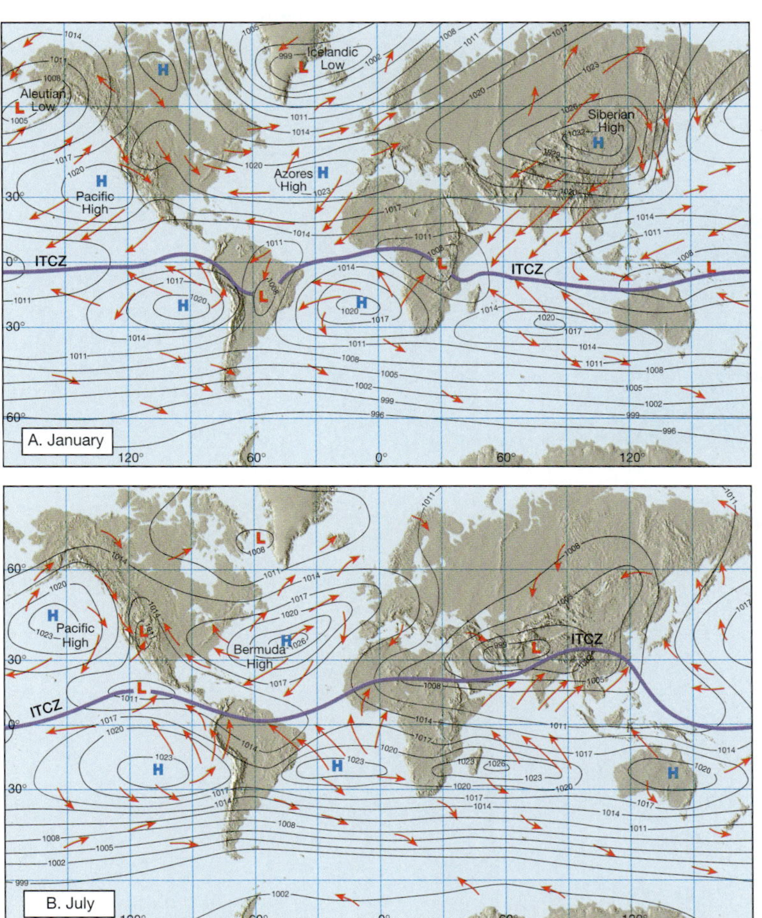

Figure 13.15 **Global distribution of air pressure for January and July.**

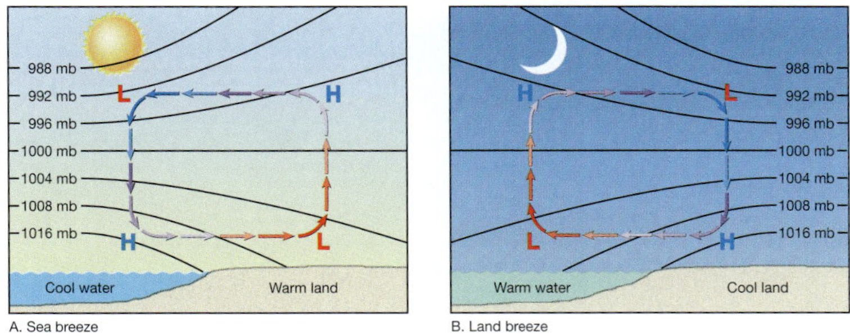

Figure 13.16 **Sea breeze and a land breeze.**

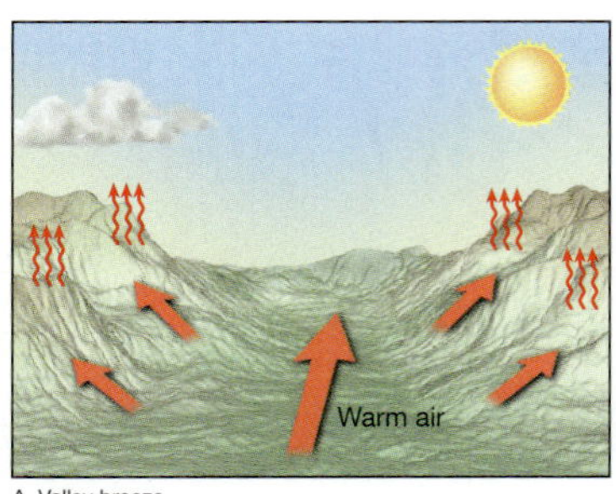

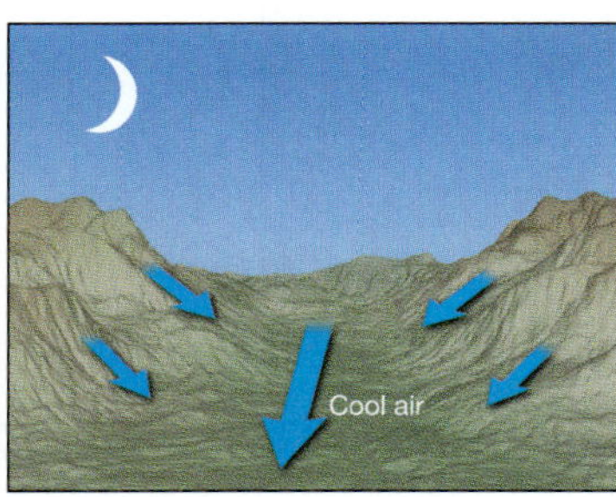

Figure 13.17 Valley and mountain breezes.

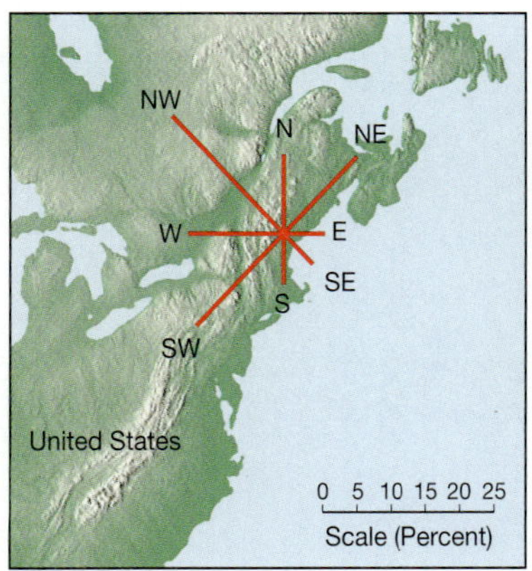

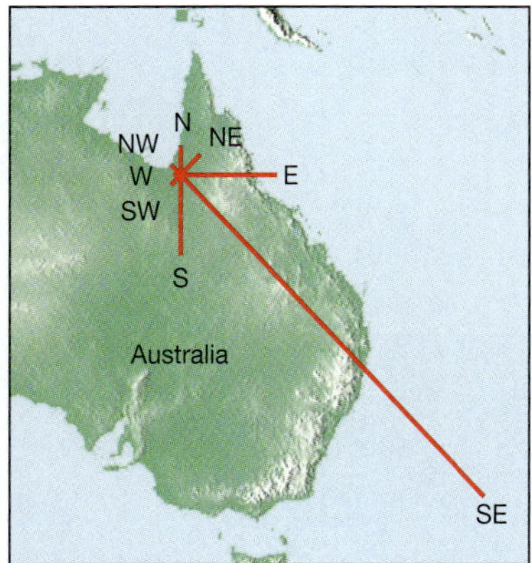

Figure 13.19 Wind roses.

NOTES:

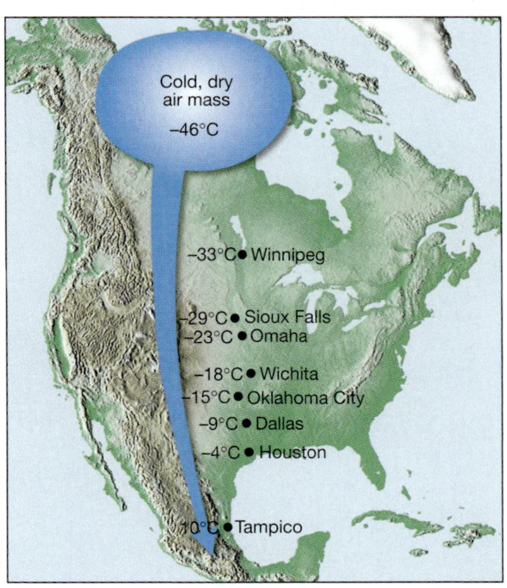

Figure 14.1 Movement of a Canadian air mass.

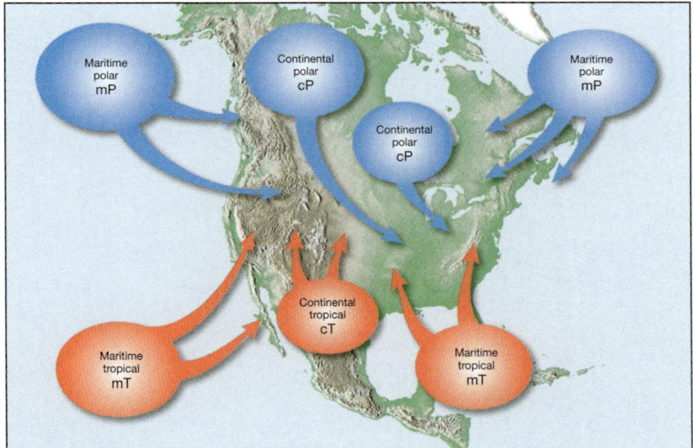

Figure 14.2 Air mass source regions.

Figure 14.3 Snowbelts of the Great Lakes region.

NOTES:

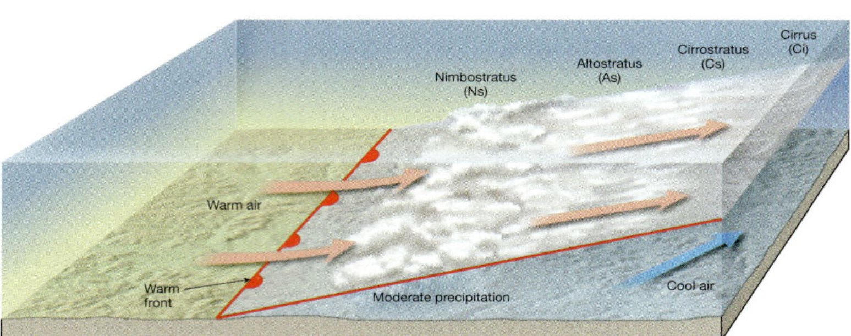

Figure 14.4 Warm front.

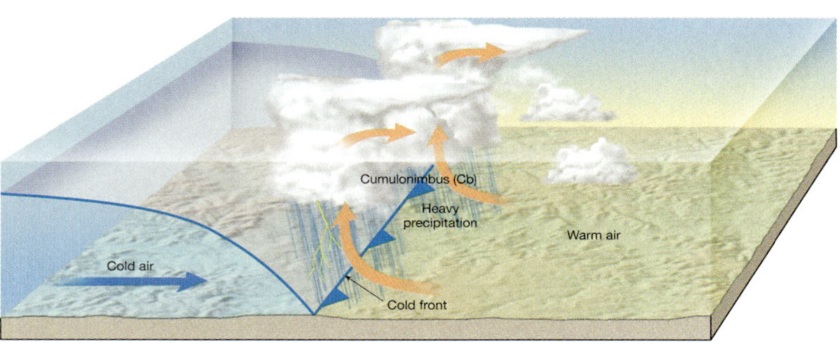

Figure 14.5 Cold front.

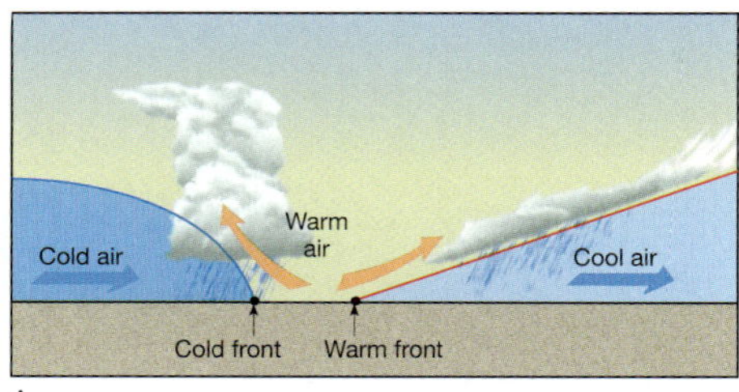

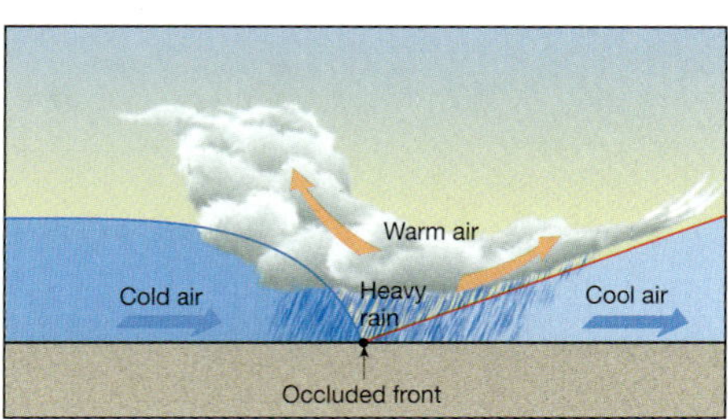

**Figure 14.6 Stages in the form-
ation of an occluded front.**

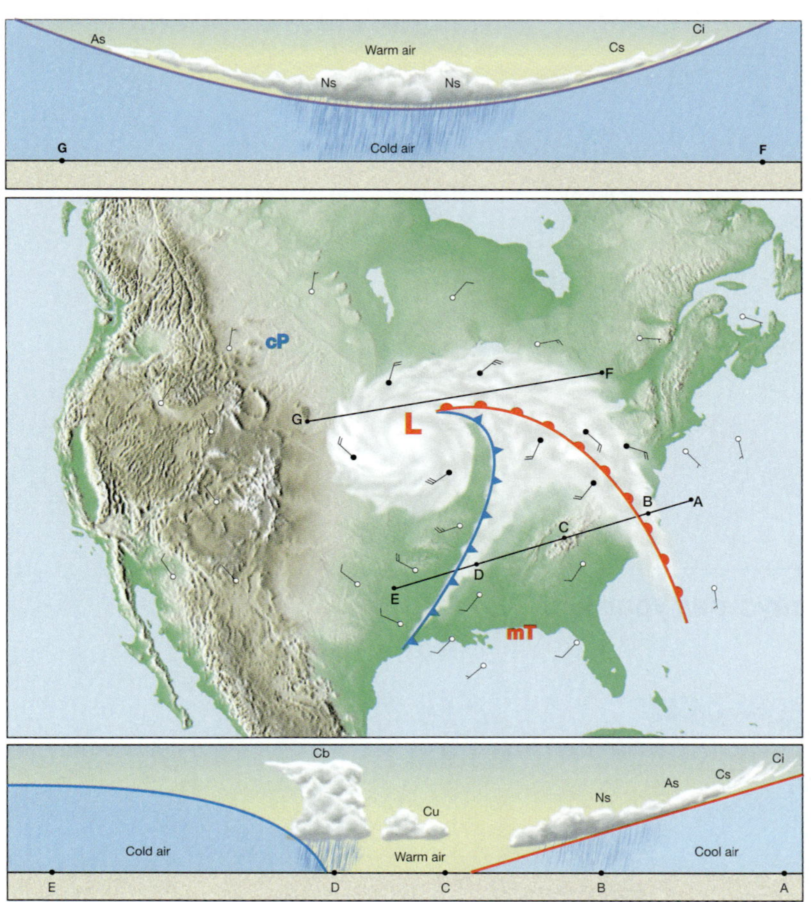

Figure 14.7 Cloud patterns asociated with a mature middle-latitude cyclone.

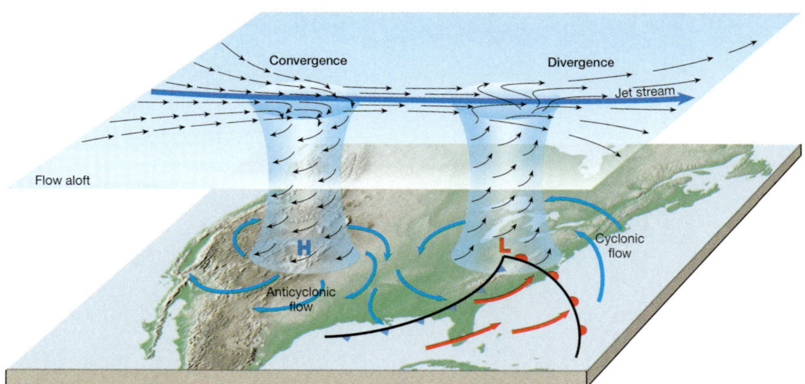

Figure 14.9 The support that divergence and convergence aloft provide to cyclonic and anticyclonic circulation at the surface.

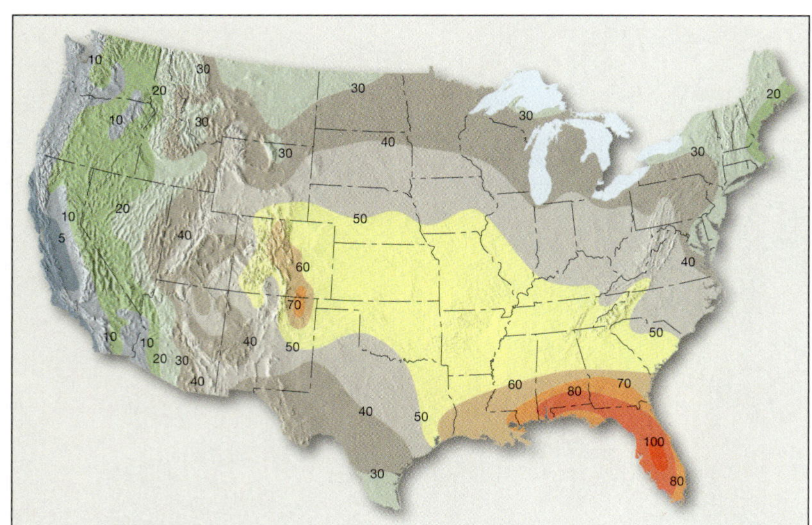

Figure 14.11 Average number of days per year with thunderstorms.

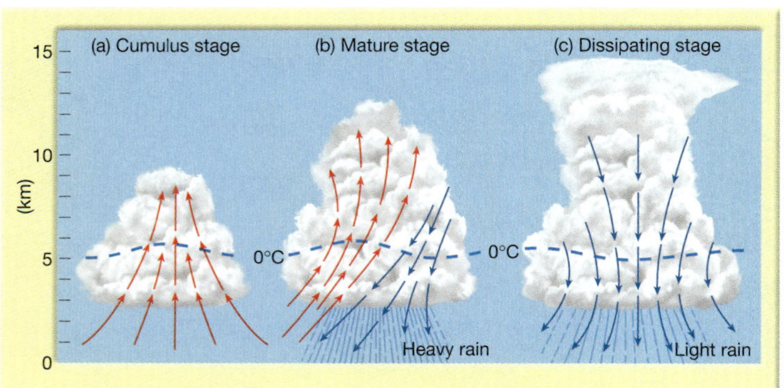

Figure 14.13 Stages in the development of a thunderstorm.

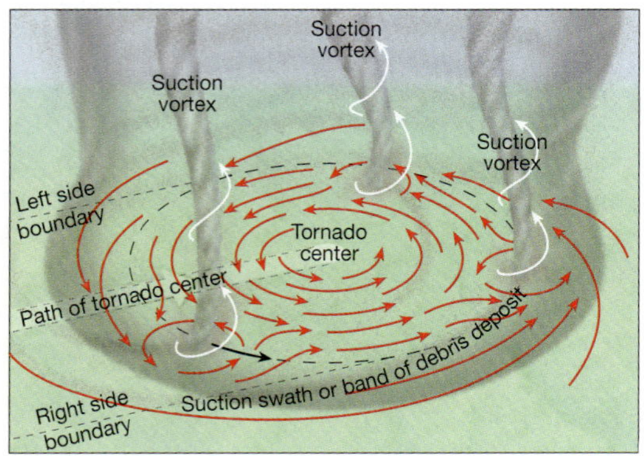

Figure 14.14 Some tornadoes have multiple suction vortices.

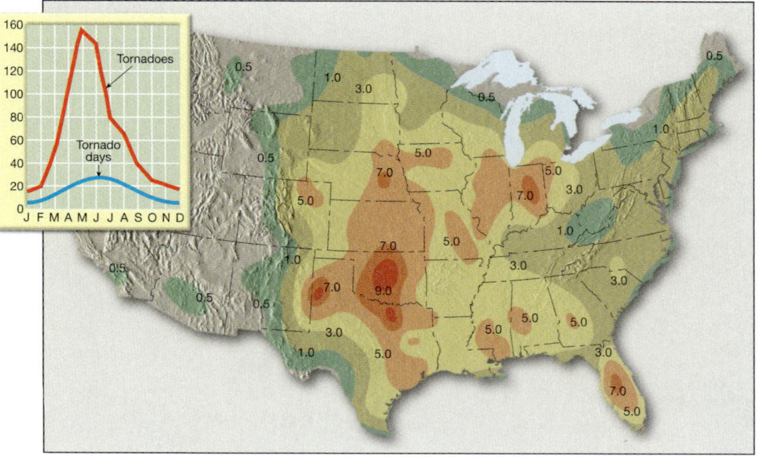

Figure 14.15 A,B,C Formation of a mesocyclone and tornado.

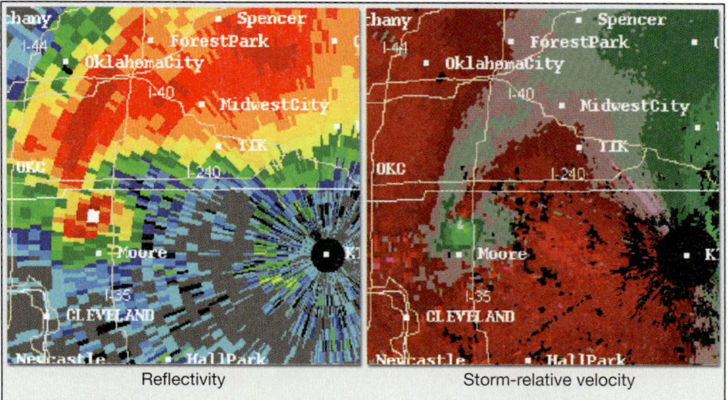

Figure 14.16 Tornado incidence per 10,000 square miles and the average number of tornadoes and tornado days each month in the U.S.

Figure 14.18 Doppler radar image of an F5 tornado.

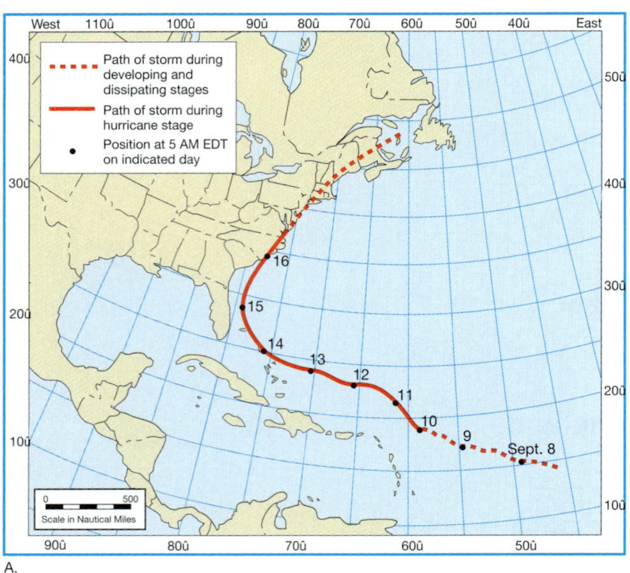

Figure 14.20 A Hurricane Floyd.

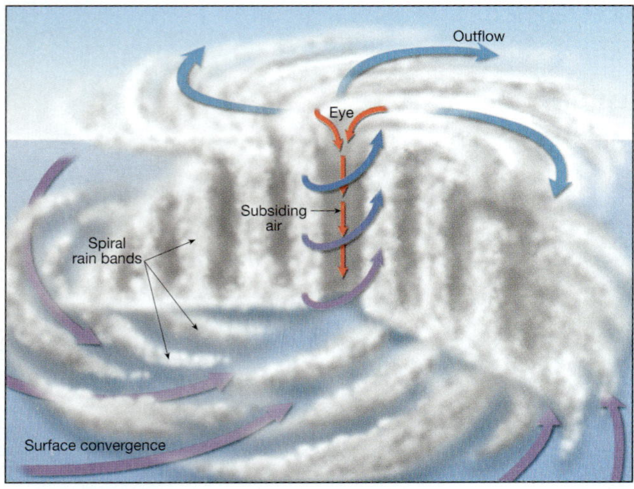

Figure 14.21 Cross section of a hurricane.

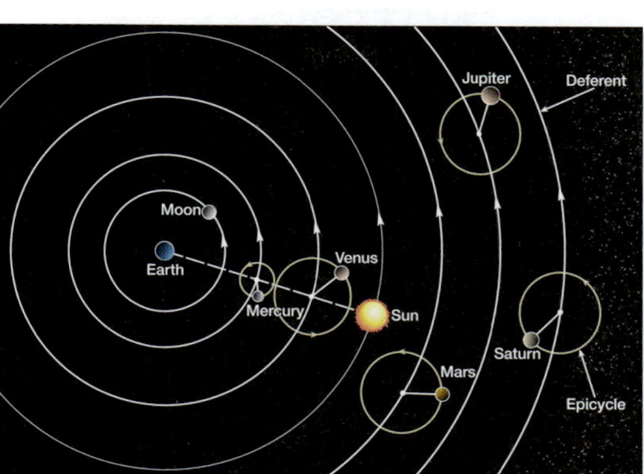

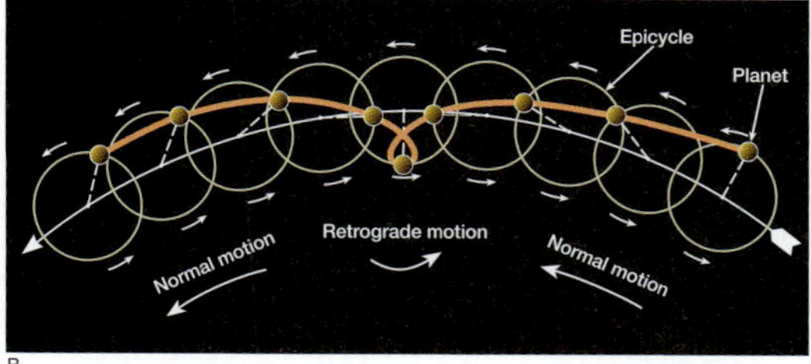

Figure 15.2 View of the universe according to Ptolemy.

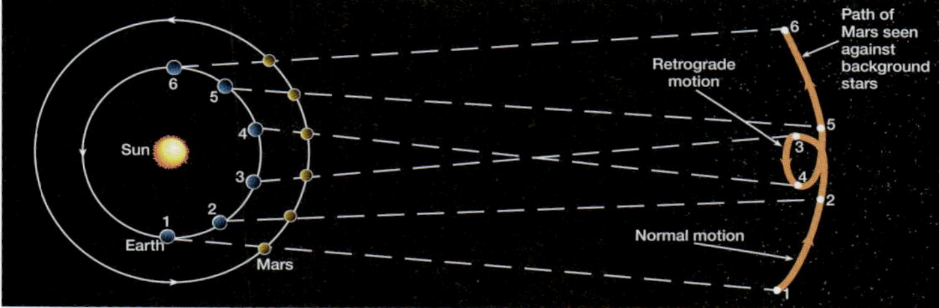

Figure 15.3 Retrograde (backward) motion of Mars.

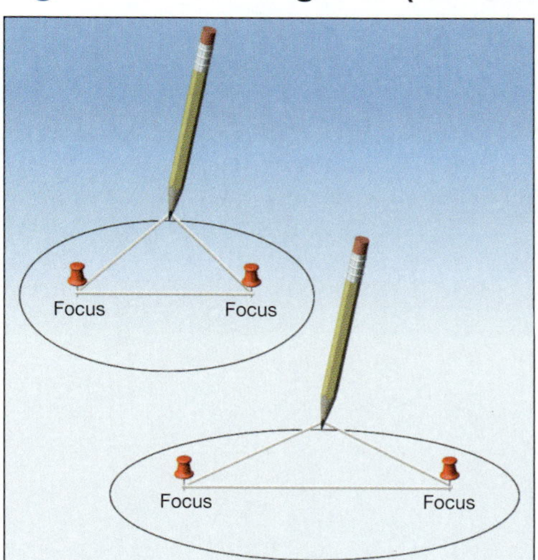

Figure 15.6 Drawing ellipses with various eccentricities.

NOTES:

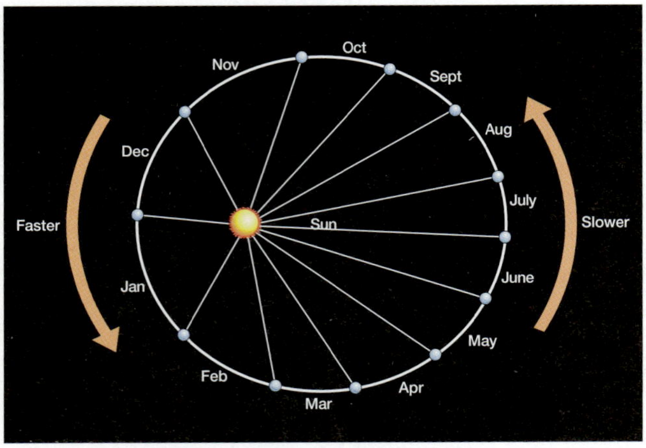

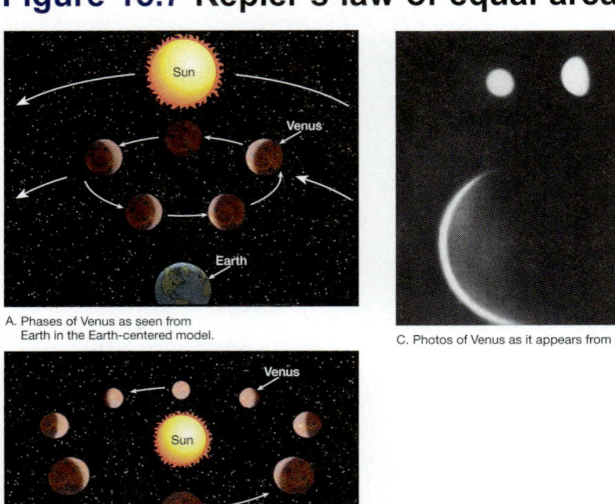

Figure 15.7 Kepler's law of equal areas.

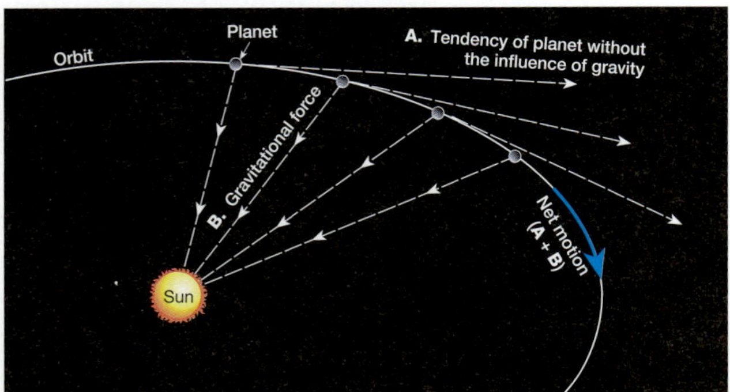

Figure 15.10 Phases of Venus.

Figure 15.12 Orbital motion of Earth and other planets.

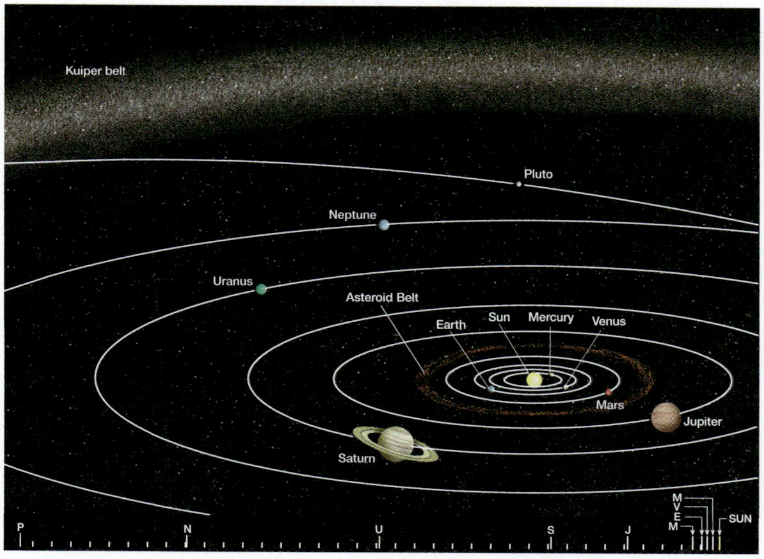

Figure 15.13 **Orbits of the planets.**

Figure 15.14 **The planets drawn to scale.**

Figure 15.15 Formation of the solar system according to the nebular hypothesis.

NOTES:

NOTES:

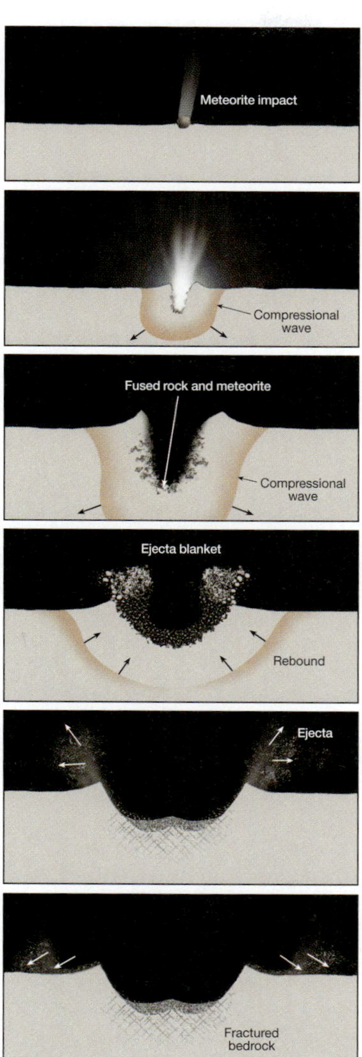

Figure 15.17 **Formation of an impact crater.**

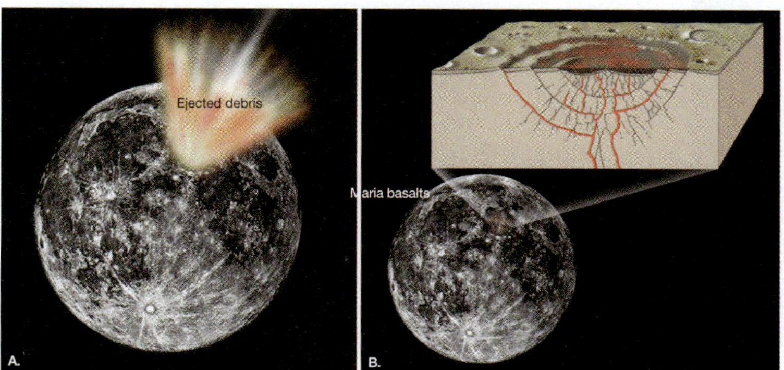

Figure 15.19 Formation of lunar maria.

NOTES:

Figure 15.26 Artist's view of Jupiter with Earth for scale.

Figure 15.29 A view of the ring system of Saturn.

Figure 15.32 Pluto and its moon Charon. Earth shown for scale.

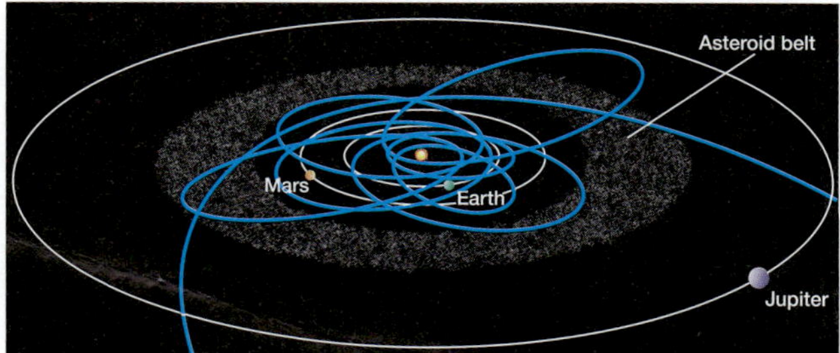

Figure 15.33 The orbits of asteroids.

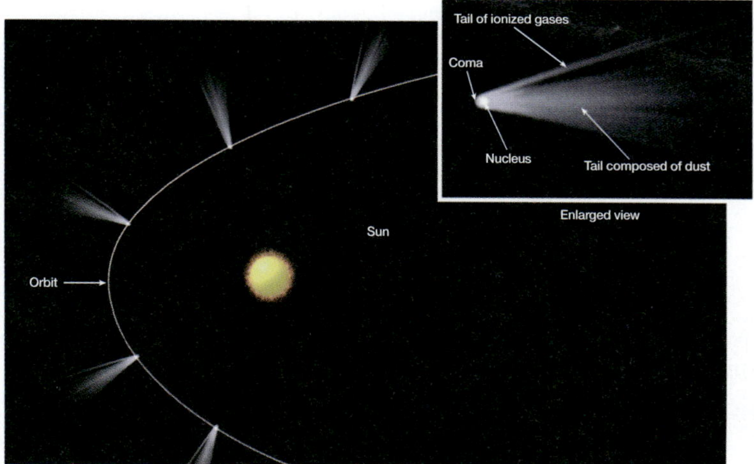

Figure 15.35 Orientation of a comet's tail as it orbits the Sun.

CHAPTER 16 - Beyond the Solar System

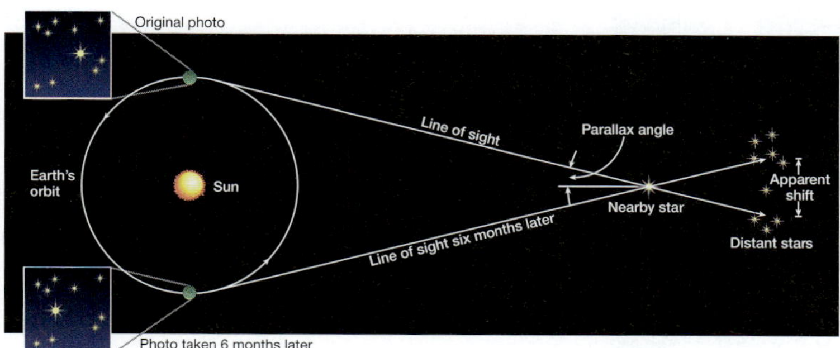

Figure 16.2 Geometry of stellar parallax.

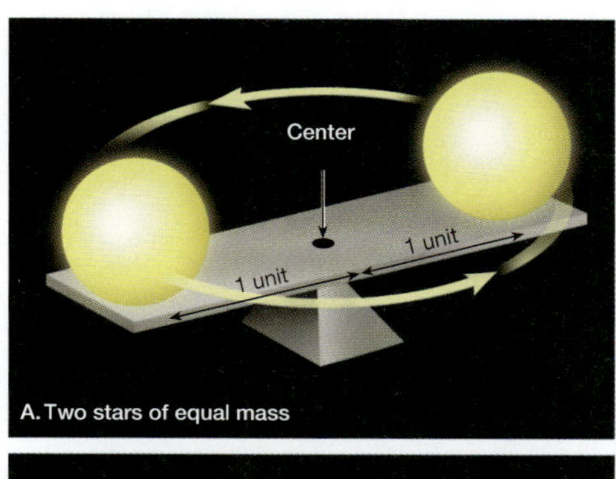

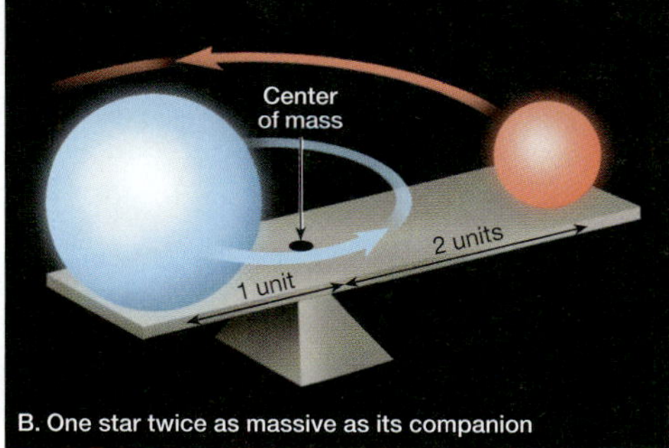

Figure 16.4 Binary stars.

NOTES:

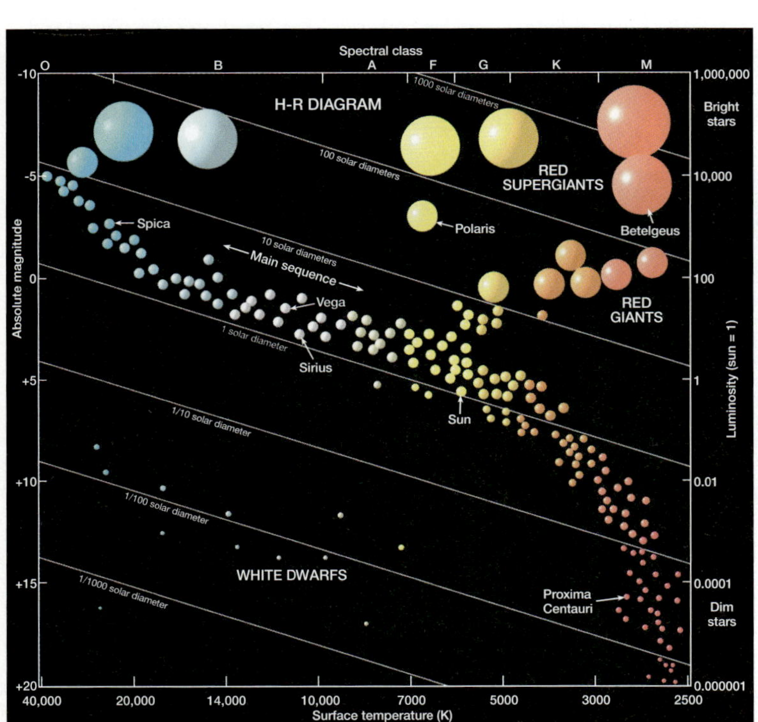

Figure 16.5 Idealized Hertzsprung-Russell diagram.

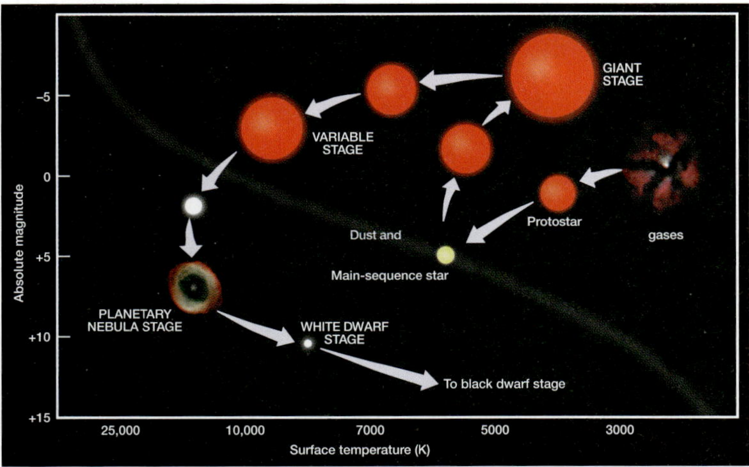

Figure 16.9 Diagram of stellar evolution on H-R diagram.

NOTES:

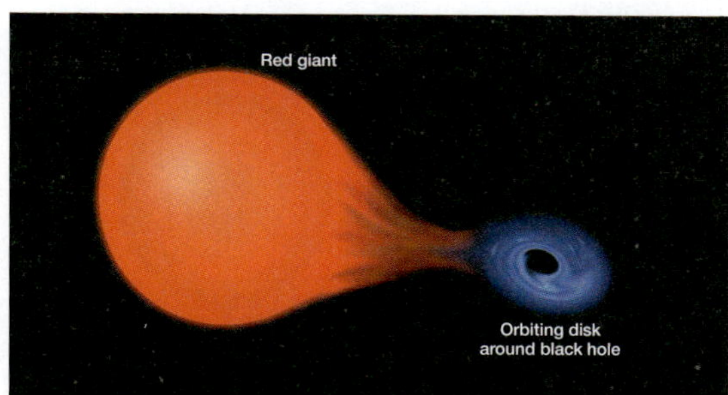

Figure 16.10 The evolutionary stages of stars having various masses.

Figure 16.14 Binary pair.

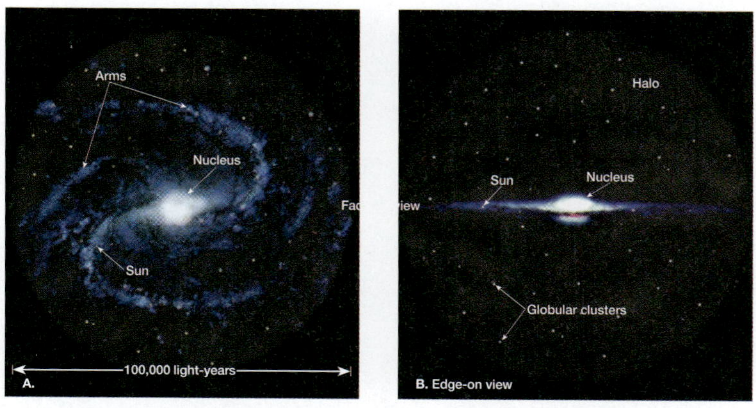

Figure 16.16 Structure of the visible portion of the Milky Way galaxy.

NOTES:

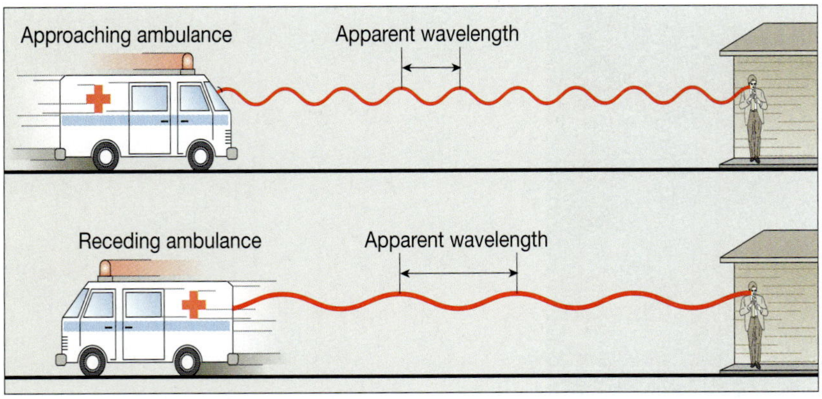

Figure 16.21 The Doppler effect.

NOTES: